Measuring & Improving Social, Environmental & Economic Productivity: Getting It Done!

Mike Dillon & John Heap

Institute of
Productivity

Published by the Institute of Productivity

in association with the

Open College Network

and the

World Confederation of Productivity Science

ISBN: 978-0-9572726-0-6

DEDICATION

This book is dedicated to all those in the productivity movement who have educated, influenced and inspired us.

Mike Dillon
John Heap

Social, Environmental & Economic Productivity: the SEE concept

The SEE-Productivity concept was developed by, and is used by the authors with permission from, the Board of Directors of the World Confederation of Productivity Science (WCPS). Any individual or organization seeking to use the SEE Productivity concept, must obtain written permission of the WCPS Board of Directors. Such permission, if granted, is not a guarantee of endorsement. To contact the Board of Directors of the World Confederation of Productivity Science, please go to www.wcps.info

Contents

ACKNOWLEDGMENTS

We want to acknowledge the help of the members of the World Confederation of Productivity Science and the European Association of National Productivity Centres whose conversations, discussions and debates have helped us think through the issues that have shaped this book.

We would also like to acknowledge the discussions with our colleagues at Grimsby Institute of Further & Higher Education who shared a passion for productivity and corporate social responsibility.

i

Preface

By Dr. M. Prakash

SOCIAL PRODUCTIVITY IN RELATION TO ECONOMIC DEVELOPMENT

The concept of 'productivity' has evolved from the simple relationship between inputs and outputs with the recognition that it is a major factor in creating improvements to the quality of life - for all peoples. It is now seen as being inextricably interwoven with current, major global issues such as sustainability, the eradication of poverty and regional imbalances in development. So, modern views of productivity are both inward-looking - at productivity as a device for improving a company's 'bottom-line' - and outward-looking – at how productivity development can help sustain organisations over the longer-term and help nations improve the health and well-being of their citizens.

Social productivity is a 'movement' that is encouraging companies to use their economic well-being (and the improvements in this well-being brought about by improved productivity) to deliver a better quality of life. Of course, some would claim that 'social productivity' is just another term for corporate social responsibility (CSR) ... but there are important differences. CSR – as practised – often concentrates on environmental issues and even when it addresses 'social' issues it often does as a form of altruism.

Social productivity is much more a mainstream business concept, aimed at bottom-line improvements ... but aimed at making those bottom-line improvements over the longer-term and using 'social improvements' as part of the process of generating those longer-term bottom-lime improvements.

Social Productivity is increasingly understood within Indian corporate culture. India has a long tradition of 'social entrepreneurship' and this tradition and experience is reflected in a number of innovative business models which are helping to create India as a world, social innovation hub. This, of course, reflects India's economic and cultural context. "While the US will be the innovator for the top one billion (of the world's population), India will become the innovation hub for the bottom five," says JayantSinha, managing director & country head, Omidyar Network, India that aims to invest up to $ 200 million in both for-profit and non-profit social enterprises in India over the next five years.

The social innovations that have changed and are changing the face of India act as models for other developing and under-developed economies. India has identified ways of successfully addressing the huge regional disparities in key economic and social indicators like income, education, access to healthcare, employment opportunities and so on. This involves both product innovation - creating products and services that are appropriate to, and can reach, different strata of the society - and process innovation – changing the ways in which certain activities are carried out to make them more relevant to the local stakeholder groups.

One example is that of the Tata Swach water purifier. Though there has been water purification technology available for many years, large numbers of Indian children die each year through a lack of clean, drinking water. Water borne diseases are responsible for twice the number of deaths as caused by AIDS in India. In spite of this, a mere 6% of urban Indian households adopt some kind of drinking water purification device, while the number in rural areas is significantly lower.

Tata identified this as a problem which needed a solution but, more importantly, needed an affordable solution. Their development work resulted in just that – an affordable form of water purification. Different versions of the product are available in urban and rural areas with versions varying in size, price and usability. Like many 'social developments', this product was the basis of a true 'win-win' situation.

Tata has generated profits from an innovative and appropriate product; the population of India has benefitted from the availability of the purified water produced and India, as a whole, has benefited from the improved health and well-being of the workforce.

This 'path to profit' through addressing specific environmental or social need is not uncommon. Another example is that of Jain Irrigation in Maharashtra adopting a similar mission of "Leave this world better than you found it". Jain Irrigation supported and created opportunities for millions of small-time farmers to improve the performance of their land; and in so doing they created improved performance and profit for the company.

Both these examples show that addressing social issues as long-term, mainstream business opportunities is a route to business success ... and improving the well-being of specific groups of societal stakeholders. This is the message of 'social productivity'.

India offer some particularly fine examples, but this is a wider issue ... that should be taken up by organisations across the globe who are willing to take the 'longer view' to economic, environmental and social sustainability.

Dr. M. PRAKASH
Principal,
Seshadripuram First Grade College.
Bangalore, India

The Getting It Done Series

This is the first in a series of books from the Institute of Productivity aimed at providing a comprehensive, practical approach to the measurement and improvement of performance and productivity, at organisational and at national level.

These books are aimed at a range of audiences – from policy-makers and strategists, through project officers and facilitators to (especially) the practitioners - those responsible for 'Getting It Done'.

The books introduce and explain relevant concepts and theory but they always take the reader through specific approaches, techniques and examples that act as a template for practical implementation.

The books are designed to be pragmatic … to give real world approaches and solutions. We have also designed the book to be brief … and to be complementary. Though each book stands alone, maximum benefit comes from applying the concepts across the series of books – Getting It (All) Done.

www.instituteofproductivity.com

The Institute of Productivity is a think-tank, publishing house and strategic consultancy focusing on the trade and business benefits of addressing all of Social, Environmental & Economic (SEE) Productivities. However, we aim to focus many of our projects and activities on social productivity since we believe that this is the 'Cinderella' of the three productivities and therefore worthy of 'special attention'.

The Institute has a particular interest in the impact of vocational education on organisational and national performance, adopting a philosophy of Productivity Action via Vocational Education (PAVE). We support the development of educational institutions that interpret vocational education widely (and deeply) since we have evidence, from our research, of the financial impact of company-wide, vocational education and training strategies. There are new models of educational institution being created to reflect this wider view of vocational education and we are keen to support such developments in pursuit of national/regional economic and social development.

We are also committed to the concept of benchmarking as a means of driving improvement, recognising that measurement is a key component of understanding. For this reason we are also committed to providing models and techniques by which the impact of development projects can be assessed before delivery. This allows funders to make rational, evidence-based decisions in where to apply limited funds in order to create maximum economic, and social, impact. The second book in this "Getting It Done" series relates to the assessment of such impact.

1 What is this thing called productivity ... and why does it matter?

Productivity is a simple concept ... but it gets complicated in practice. Expressed at its most simple, it is the ratio of what we produce (outputs) to the resources we use in that production (inputs).

It is not the same as 'production'. If you increase production (output) but your inputs go up proportionally (as they are most likely to do), your productivity has stayed the same ...

.... and if you increase productivity but your inputs go up proportionally more (perhaps because you had to pay overtime rates) your productivity will have gone down.

So, when we attempt to improve productivity, we are normally looking to:

Improve the volume of (quality) output without a corresponding increase in costs

or

Reduce costs whilst maintaining output levels

This simple definition of productivity works at the level of the organisation ....

... where the productivity of the organisation is the ratio of the outputs from the organisation to the inputs (the various resources) it uses to make those outputs

..... and it works at the regional or national level ... where the productivity of the region or nation is the ratio of the outputs produced by the region or nation to the inputs used to make those outputs.... and it is the state of national productivity that determines whether a country is competitive globally.

This simple definition also works well when both the outputs and inputs are tangible and can be easily counted. However, it soon becomes more complex.

Let's take a simple example .... which like our definition, soon starts to lose its simplicity.

Mary Jane works from home so that she can look after her two young children. She recently saw a kit for making cushions, made a few and decided she could make some money from it. Though she was very slow when starting off, and though she does all her sewing by hand, Mary Jane can now make about 40 cushions a week and her sister has started selling them at local craft fairs.

Mary Jane's output in a month is 160 cushions and her input of time to make those 160 cushions is 100 hours.

Her productivity is therefore **160 over 100 = 1.6 cushions per hour**.

(Of course we don't know whether this is good or bad – because we have nothing to compare it to - but at least it is better than when she first started.)

Mary Jane works out how to do things better without the kit. She can complete each cushion faster and make 200 cushions in a month without putting in any more time.

Her productivity is now **200 over 100 = 2 cushions per hour**.

This is a productivity increase of (40 / 160) x 100 = 25%

Then, Mary Jane and her sister (who is enjoying the money she is making from selling these cushions) decide to buy a sewing machine between them to make Mary Jane even more productive.

Soon Mary Jane is up to 400 cushions a month - again with putting no more time in.

Mary Jane's productivity is now **400 over 100 = 4 cushions per hour**

Everything seems to be moving in the right direction!

But let's look at this from a **business** point of view ... after all, Mary Jane is running a (very small) business.

Mary Jane started selling the cushions at £10 each.

Her original productivity was therefore (1.6 x 10) = £16 of cushions per hour

(We often measure inputs in terms of their cost as it allows us to combine a number of inputs using a common measure - literally, a common currency!)

Otherwise it would be hard to put into the productivity ratio a total of units of energy, hours of labour, tonnes of materials .... and add them into a total for inputs consumed. This is possible with £ of energy, £ of labour and £ of materials.

Of course if we want to compare productivity over time, we have to convert such monetary measures to a common baseline so that we strip out the effects of inflation ... you see, it is getting complicated!)

And with her sewing machine her productivity appears to be (4 x 10) or £40 of cushions produced per hour. This means that Mary Jane and her sister get more profit. But they've had to pay out for the sewing machine .... the production process now has more inputs. ... there is 'capital equipment' involved. If we put this money into the productivity ratio the figures change.

(Of course we would have to decide on the useful life of the sewing machine and therefore how much to charge to the business each month.)

Unfortunately, as well, Mary Jane's sister is having trouble selling all the additional cushions. She is just about managing but she has had to lower the price to £8 each to ensure they all sell.

This affects the output of the business (if we express it in monetary terms) and therefore the productivity.

It's getting more complicated ..... and remember this is a very small and very simple business. Of course, later we will come back to the concept of productivity, and how it can be measured (and improved): for now, though let us just accept that it is a simple concept in principle, but more complicated in practice.

In fact, we are shortly going to complicate it even more. However, let us first of all remind ourselves why we need to be thinking about, and improving productivity.

Why is Productivity Important?

Well, essentially because improving productivity is the only way to add extra value and make a business more profitable in the longer-term. Productivity increases the size of the cake that is shared out ... rather than just trying to slice up the cake in different proportions.

If we do more - but do not improve our productivity - our costs (inputs) go up in line with our outputs. This might be OK if we are profitable now .... but it won't give us additional margins and added value. This is true for all organisations. If we want to make the organisation more effective - and make a bigger contribution for our shareholders, our owners, our members, our community (whilst, of course, remaining competitive) - then we have to raise productivity.

The nature of the environment in which most organisations now operate requires them to compete on a global level ...... to become, and remain, competitive in such an environment requires a long-term commitment to addressing the issues of productivity.

At the national level, perhaps it is even more important. Paul Krugman (Krugman, 1992) once famously said ... "Productivity isn't everything, but in the long run it is almost everything. A country's ability to improve its standard of living over time depends almost entirely on its ability to raise its output per worker. World War II veterans came home to an economy that doubled its productivity over the next 25 years; as a result, they found themselves achieving living standards their parents had never imagined. Vietnam veterans came home to an economy that raised its productivity less than 10 percent in 15 years; as a result, they found themselves living no better - and in many cases worse - than their parents."

Increased productivity is what generates additional wealth without increasing inflation: it is thus the way in which a nation can create real, additional wealth. It is how a nation can become better able to finance the health, hygiene, housing, educational and social support systems it might desire for its citizens. However one defines 'better off', it is productivity improvement that makes nations – and their peoples – better off.

Productivity is important in all sectors of the economy and in all types of organisation. Over the last couple of decades, it has been 'adopted' by the public sector in many countries keen to show that they are accountable for the money they spend (which normally comes from taxation).

For example, in 2010 the UK Government's Department of Heath set up the Quality, Innovation, Productivity and Prevention (QIPP) programme to …

"ensure that each pound spent is used to bring maximum benefit and quality of care to patients."

The programme is designed to be a 'transformational' programme and aims to make up to 20 billion pounds of efficiency savings by 2014- 2015 … to be re-invested in frontline care.

Take another example – one that reflects the growing importance of issues such as food, energy and water security. The world has a growing population and this population is likely to grow for the foreseeable future. At the same time, we are seeing the growth of cities, the migration of rural people to these urban areas in the pursuit of work, and the lowering of the landmass given over to agriculture. This is a recipe for disaster – or a call for greater agricultural productivity.

We have to see a rise in food production yields … and because the growing cities take more and more water away from agriculture, we need a massive rise in water productivity – in terms of 'crop per drop'.

Adding in complications

We have said that productivity is most simply expressed as the ratio of outputs to inputs. However, not all of our outputs are good! In most industries, some of the output will be in the form of waste, scrap, emissions and pollutants. In addition to any effects these have on the environment and the planet, they cost the business money.

Environmental Productivity

Environmental Productivity (sometimes referred to as Green Productivity) is a term increasingly used to describe an approach to productivity improvement where we address these 'negative outputs' and simultaneously make our business and our environment better. This can be done by looking at our waste and seeing what we can do to reduce it ... but it is much more effective when we look at the whole process of producing our goods or services and see what can be done to re-design the product and/or the process to avoid creating waste (and those other negatives) in the first place.

Green productivity has been enthusiastically promoted by the Asian Productivity Organisation and there are various resources on the APO website relating to green productivity. (See www.apo-tokyo.org)

Where we cannot avoid using natural resources (including energy), we have to use them more efficiently so that we do less harm to our environment (and incur less cost to our organisation).

In *The World is Flat*, Thomas Friedman (2005) observed the dramatic changes that technology has stimulated throughout the world. The global enterprise playing field has been levelled and access to information has empowered individuals and groups. Friedman updated his "flat world" premise in his (2008) book, *Hot, Flat, and Crowded*. He writes, "... creating the tools, systems, energy sources, and ethics that will allow the planet to grow in cleaner, more sustainable ways is going to be the biggest challenge of our lifetime."

Similarly, social productivity is a concept that - like environmental productivity - applies at a number of levels - such as the sharing of wealth at a national - or even a global - level. (The word 'social' has become so embroiled in the wider phrase of 'social media': we need to reclaim it and treat 'social productivity' as more than a term representing how quickly and how often I can converse with my Twitter followers!)

Any productivity improvement project will affect a range of stakeholders .... we have already mentioned the owners and managers of an organisation, employees, suppliers, customers and so on. The concept of social productivity extends to cover all these stakeholders.

In an interconnected global context, people are becoming more aware that we are destroying our environment, depleting our natural resources, and widening the societal gaps in wealth and well-being. These outcomes challenge the realised value of "productive" activity.

More lately we have begun to realise that the 'old order' will not necessarily continue. The economic crisis of 2009-2011 has made people think about the nature of economic realities in zero (or negative) growth conditions.

If we are to go through a prolonged period of low economic growth, how do we cope with an increasing global population and rising levels of unemployment, in addition to the existing (but growing) problems of rising global temperatures and reduced supplies of fossil fuels. Clearly we have to rethink one of the 'old truths' … that economic growth will solve (or at the very least ameliorate) such problems.

Returning to first principles, we stated right at the beginning of this chapter that productivity is expressed most simply as the ratio of a system's outputs to its inputs. Our heightened awareness now demands that we take into account the fact that, in many cases (and particularly in a low growth context) the net result of productivity might be wealth inequality and social damage.

This is, of course, equally true in developing countries which see economic growth as the means to improve the well-being of their citizens. However, unbridled and unbalanced economic productivity growth often benefits the few rather than the many, and often results in poor environmental performance as emissions and pollution increase.

So, we do need a balanced approach which addresses all of social, environmental and economic productivity.

Some ethical consumers, concerned environmentalists, global NGOs and so on are lobbying for change. Companies are moving from concentrating on stakeholder *value* (how much money they make for their shareholders) to concentrating on stakeholder *values,* recognizing that there are multiple stakeholders whose values sometimes conflict.

The world, more generally, must commit to facilitating the management of the outcomes of productivity efforts, and the mitigation of its unintended consequences.

The Triple Bottom Line

Elkington (1999) coined the term 'triple bottom line' (TBL) to represent this emerging focus on the three factors of social, environmental and economic added value. This concept has been modified over time and is now often summarised as People, Planet, Profit.

The TBL has developed into an accounting framework that incorporates the three dimensions of performance: social, environmental and financial. However, finding a common unit of measurement is one challenge. For many measures (including many productivity measures), we attempt to convert measures into monetary units, since this offers a consistent and comparable basis of measurement and understanding. However, this is not always possible – we will look at the challenges of measuring these various performance/productivity factors in subsequent chapters.

Shared Value

A similar concept is contained within the term 'shared value' to refer to business activity which involves creating economic value in a way that *also* creates value for society by addressing its needs and challenges. (Porter & Kramer, 2011).

Porter & Kramer suggest that a key reason that social issues are normally excluded from business thinking is that economists have made the case that to provide benefit to society, companies must temper their financial success. i.e. it costs organisations money to consider social benefit.

However, Porter & Kramer suggest that this is due to incomplete thinking. They suggest that addressing the concept of shared value actually helps define markets and, further, that a failure to address such needs may create internal costs for firms – wasted energy and materials, costly accidents and remedial education and training to make up for the inadequacies of standard public education.

SEE productivity

Members of the World Confederation of Productivity Science have been instrumental in the development and promotion of environmental or green productivity as part of the evolution from 'traditional' views of productivity to consideration of the multiple views represented by the triple bottom line. (Tuttle & Heap, 2008)

(WCPS – see Footnote at the end of this Chapter - is a global think-tank on productivity based in Montreal, Canada.(http://www.wcps.info).

The WCPS became convinced that these three factors had to be viewed holistically and had to be viewed as a business issue, not as an 'add-on' issue of corporate social responsibility. At the World Productivity Congress in South Africa in 2008, the WCPS launched their concept of SEE productivity, reflecting this wider recognition that, to be sustainable in the longer-term, organisations, nations and regions need to improve all of social, environmental and economic productivities so that their operations are socially equitable, environmentally bearable AND economically viable (see Figure 1-1).

What we do in pursuit of growth and wealth must be economically viable, but also must be environmentally bearable and socially equitable.

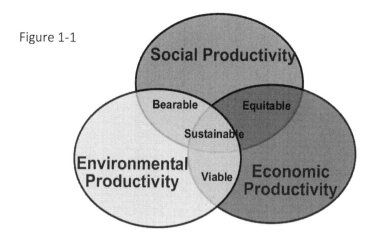

Figure 1-1

Social Productivity

Bearable   Equitable

Sustainable

Environmental
Productivity   Viable

Economic
Productivity

From Accounting to Accountability

A number of factors are coming together to create what – hopefully – might be some form of 'perfect storm'. The concept of global warming has led to a strong focus (but weaker action) on environmental issues and whether or not global warming is actually happening … and whether or not it is man-made … any rational human being must be able to see the speed at which we are using up the earth's resources … and the growing demand for those resources …. and the need, therefore, to use them more efficiently.

This focus on the environment and on conserving resources has resulted in a wider, growing agenda of many organisations to act as responsible citizens – to be aware of their corporate social responsibility (CSR). The concept of SEE reminds us that it is not a public relations issue – it is a business issue. It must be a true move from accounting to accountability. Improving social, environmental and economic productivities puts a focus on the top line of the productivity ratio – in terms of exploring the 'value' that we create for our various stakeholder groups … and this exploration then directly affects the bottom line.

Is addressing SEE productivity a good business strategy?

So, the concept of SEE productivity needs to be adopted at national and at organisational level.

As above, one can see the clear advantages for government of improved social and environmental productivity – less cost for the same levels of service/protection. It is a clear 'business improvement' issue.

For organisations too, we are suggesting that SEE should be regarded as a business issue, not an add-on 'altruistic' issue. We have so far suggested that we believe there is a 'pay-back' in terms of longer-term sustainability.

It would be useful (and helpful) if there was evidence to back up this belief.

A recent piece of research compared a matched sample of 180 US-based companies, 90 of which were classified as high-sustainability and another 90 as low-sustainability. This classification was based on the adoption of environmental, social, and governance (ESG) policies in the 1990s that reinforced a cultural commitment to sustainability. The environmental policies related to such factors as carbon emissions, green supply-chain policies and energy and water-efficiency strategies. Social policies included internal issues such as diversity and equal-opportunity targets, work-life balance, and health & safety improvement, alongside external issues such as corporate citizenship commitments, business ethics, and human-rights criteria. Finally, other policies accounted for related to customers, product risk and customer health and safety.

Amongst the sample studies, the high-sustainability companies had adopted an average of 40% of these policies early on, while their counterparts had adopted only 10%. The two sets of companies were selected to be identical in terms of financial performance in the early 1990s, in order to examine the long-term performance effects of a culture of sustainability.

The research found, not surprisingly, that high-sustainability organisations were characterised by a governance structure that explicitly and directly took into account the environmental and social performance of the company, in addition to financial performance. These companies were more likely to make executive compensation a function of environmental, social, and external perception (eg customer satisfaction) metrics and were more likely to measure and report on environmental and social metrics in addition to their financial results.

Importantly, these differences in behaviour are reflected in differences in financial performance. Over an 18-year period, the high-sustainability companies dramatically outperformed the low-sustainability ones in terms of both stock market and accounting measures. The annual above-market average return for the high-sustainability sample was 4.8% higher than for their counterparts and with lower volatility.

The high-sustainability companies also performed much better as measured by return on equity and return on assets. (Eccles, Ioannou & Serafeim, 2011)

A reading of this relatively brief summary might lead one to (sensibly) ask the question of 'correlation versus causality' - does the research go on to establish that there is a causal link between an organisation adopting a high-sustainability stance, together with associated practices, and the increased business performance? The authors address this question in the paper and while – quite correctly – being somewhat cautious, they do comment that their evidence does in fact suggest a causal relationship. They also suggest that high sustainability organisations out-perform low-sustainability organisations only in the longer-term; adopting a high sustainability stance is not a recipe with which to address short-term competitiveness.

Of course there is a tendency for firms to 'talk up' the importance of environmentalism and sustainability.

14

The 2011 version of the annual "Sustainability & Innovation Global Executive Study' carried out (on 4,700 corporate leaders) by MIT Sloan Management Review and The Boston Consulting Group reported that 66% of companies said sustainability is necessary for competitiveness. This was up from 55% in 2010. However, the study also reported that sustainability ranks only eighth in importance among management agenda items. (MIT, 2011)

So, we have slightly conflicting evidence. There is quite a bit of 'game-playing' amongst corporate leaders 'talking the executive talk' in relation to environmentalism but failing to deliver on the promise. There is, though, some firmer evidence that those who do also 'walk the walk' are seeing business benefits.

Currently most of this activity relates to environmental productivity; little, unfortunately, relates to social productivity. We, in the Institute of Productivity, believe that addressing environmental as well as economic factors does pay off if one takes the longer view … and we believe that evidence is emerging to confirm that belief. These are indeed business issues. Addressing SEE productivity addresses the needs of stakeholders and the longer-term stability and sustainability of 'the business'.

The Future?

The pundits keep reminding us that the only thing constant is change.

All sorts of external factors - the availability of raw materials, government policies, legislation, the availability of capital, interest rates (need I go on?) - have an impact on organisations.

Looking at our productivity (in all its forms) enables us to understand and then improve the ratio of our outputs to our inputs - to add more value, to reduce 'negative value' and to become both stronger and more sustainable.

A fit, lean, efficient and flexible organisation has much more ability to cope with external change.

A nation that addresses its social, environmental and economic productivity is similarly likely to be 'on the ball' in relation to its competitive position in world trade.

Footnote: World Confederation of Productivity Science

The World Confederation of Productivity Science is a global NGO promoting and supporting the development of productivity science.

In 1968, a number of productivity organizations resolved to form the World Confederation of Productivity Science (WCPS). These founding organizations were :

- the Institute of Work Study Practitioners, in the United Kingdom

- the Australian Institute of Industrial Engineers

- the Irish Work Study Institute

- the Work Study Association of South Africa

- the Indian Institution of Work Study.

The Confederation formally came into existence in March, 1969. The 'architect' of its creation - and its first President - was Dr. J.E.Faraday.

Since those days, the confederation has grown substantially to link together over 5o countries.

Today, there are two primary Divisions of the Confederation:

- The World Network of Productivity Organizations (WNPO) consists of the WCPS Network Partners and other affiliated bodies. Network Partners are organizations that share the aims of WCPS and have agreed to be a formal component of the confederation. Most of them are national productivity organisations. Peter Watkins is currently President of WNPO (peterfwatkins@gmail,com)

- The Fellows of the World Academy of Productivity Science (WAPS) are individuals who have been recognized for their contribution to productivity science and to the work of the Confederation. Regional Co-ordinators act on behalf of the Academy in specific geographic regions. Tom Tuttle is the current President of WAPS (tctuttle1@verizon.net).

The WCPS is committed to promoting the broad and inclusive concept of SEE (Social, Environmental & Economic) productivity, in support of its mission which is "Peace and Prosperity through Productivity".

The Confederation aims to be structurally and organizationally 'light' and to use the power of the network to influence, to persuade, to educate and to inform with the aim of promoting productivity science and productivity enhancement at a global level.

John Heap, managing director of the Institute of Productivity, is the current President of WCPS.

See http://www.wcps.info for more information.

References

Eccles, Ioannou & Serafeim (2011)
The Impact of a Corporate Culture of Sustainability on Corporate
Behavior and Performance
http://www.hbs.edu/research/pdf/12-035.pdf
Accessed January, 2012

Elkington, J. (1999).
Triple bottom-line reporting: looking for balance.
Australian CPA, 69(2), 18-21

Friedman, T.L. (2005)
The World Is Flat :A Brief History of the Twenty-first Century
Farrar, Straus and Giroux

Friedman, T.L. (2008)
Why We Need a Green Revolution - and How It Can Renew America
Picador

Krugman, P. (1992)
The Age of Diminished Expectations: US economic policy in the 1980s
MIT Press

MIT *Sloan Management Review* / Boston Consulting Group (2011)
Third Annual Sustainability Global Executive Survey: Sustainability –
The 'Embracers Seize Advantage)
Research Report, Winter 2011

Porter, M.E. & Kramer, M.R (2011)
Creating Shared Value
Harvard Business Review, Jan-Feb 2011

Tuttle, T.C & Heap, J.P. (2008)
Green Productivity: Moving the Agenda
International Journal of Productivity & Performance Management, vol
57, Issue 1

2 Social productivity

Though we in the Institute of Productivity subscribe wholeheartedly to the SEE concept and the need for organisations and nations to address all of social, environmental and economic productivities, we aim to focus many of our projects and activities on social productivity. We believe that this is the 'Cinderella' of the three productivities and therefore worthy of 'special attention'. We would also like to think that we could help move the 'corporate social responsibility' movement to include 'social' issues in their focus and actions as well as in their title!

The concept of social productivity is very new and, so far, there is no general consensus on what it is (much less on the kinds of measures that might be appropriate to represent it). However, without actually (quite) defining it, we can say that it is concerned with the way in which business and productive activity impacts on social issues and well-being.

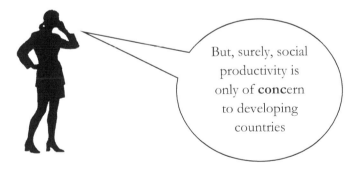

But, surely, social productivity is only of **conc**ern to developing countries

First thoughts might lead us to assume that 'social productivity' is an issue for developing countries. (If only they would act fairly and equitably - more like the developed countries - we might end poverty and ….). However the evidence suggests this is certainly not true.

For a start, there is a long tradition of commercial organisations engaging with social issues – from John Cadbury setting up the Cadbury business in 1879 because he saw 'chocolate' as a form of social reform countering the ills of alcohol consumption and its effect on poverty (Cheetham, 2008). However the examples of such 'social responsibility' we can identify are 'the exceptions that prove the rule', their very rarity showing that business, in general, has always prioritised the 'bottom line'. Even with the development of the CSR movement in recent years, this has remained so across several decades and through changes in political power.

For example, in the UK for much of the last two decades, there was a 'left wing' government (at least nominally in the sense that the labour party is the traditional left-of-centre party in the UK). One might have expected a lessening of income differentials, greater equity and a reduction in 'poverty'. However this did not happen.

In fact in this period, this did not happen in the wider world. Real disposable household incomes increased by an average 1.7% a year in OECD countries. In a large majority of them, however, the household incomes of the richest 10% grew faster than those of the poorest 10%, widening income inequality. (OECD 2011)

The same is true in most of the 'emerging economies', all of whom have levels of income inequality significantly higher than the OECD average (though some show signs of addressing the issue).

Brazil, Indonesia and, on some indicators, Argentina have recorded significant progress in reducing inequality over the past 20 years. By contrast, China, India, the Russian Federation and South Africa have all become less equal over time and inequality levels in Argentina and Brazil do remain high. Inequality in South Africa and Russia has also reached high levels. (OECD 2011)

So increasing economic productivity (which did occur) is not always reflected in increased social productivity.

The Bottom of the Pyramid

There have, of course, been some major 'breakthroughs' in looking at the way in which business impacts on social issues. There have been fewer 'breakthroughs' in looking at this issue as a mainstream business issue, rather than sidelining it – as can (but, of course, need not necessarily) happen when it is packaged as part of corporate social responsibility.

One major work was The Fortune at the Bottom of the Pyramid (Prahalad, 2004) which suggested that, far from being a problem to be solved, the poor actually represent a vast, untapped market.

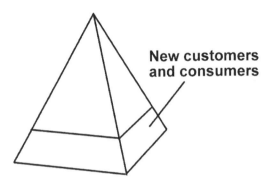

It went on to say that inclusive forms of capitalism need to be devised that engage with these people in new forms of partnership that create private-sector competition, as distinct from the more usual village and shanty-town monopolies controlled by local slum lords. Alleviating poverty then becomes a business development rather than an aid process.

Unfortunately such thinking is all too rare. However it does help us refine our thinking on social productivity. We can now come close to a definition by saying that social productivity is concerned with the distribution of wealth raised by economic performance to stakeholder communities in ways which raise their general well-being.

We talked in Chapter 1 about the growing agenda of many organisations to act as responsible citizens – to be aware of their corporate social responsibility (CSR).

The Effects of the Global Economic Crisis

This concept of 'responsible citizens' is important – recent austerity measures forced on nations as part of the global economic crisis have forced countries to re-evaluate the way in which 'social' services and 'welfare' programmes are provided and funded …. ironically addressing not only 'traditional' issues such as poverty and education but also the new issues created by the unbalanced approach taken to improved economic productivity over the last 20 years which, as we have seen has resulted in increased income differentials from the poor to the rich and increased social dissatisfaction.

In the UK, through a long period of increased national wealth, not only have these income differentials risen but health inequalities have remained stubbornly large, employers have continued to complain about a lack of basic employment skills and criminal re-offending rates have remained shockingly high (Commission on 2020 Public Services, 2010)

The commission goes on to call for a new model for providing social service and a new form of partnership between citizens and local and national government leading to:

- Citizen engagement in determining local priorities and shaping service solutions, with neighbourhood integration and commissioning.
- Visible and accountable local governance, with city and county mayors acting as catalyst, funder and regulator of public services.
- A 'more for less' deal with Whitehall, based on less money and more control for localities negotiating autonomy and service integration at different speeds.

In effect, the Commission is calling for improved social productivity.

24

Good Practice at National Level

Some nations are experimenting with social productivity schemes – often unheralded.

In 1998 (well before Social Productivity became a commonly-used term) the Government of Jordan launched their Social Productivity Program (SPP) to address the problems of poverty and unemployment. This was firstly intended to make an immediate and visible impact on the living conditions of the poor, towards the goal of providing universal access to good public infrastructure and services. Second, it was intended to make an immediate impact on the incomes of the poor, towards the goal of lifting all Jordanian households above the poverty line. Third, it was intended to assist the poor in obtaining productive employment, towards the goal of creating sustainable incomes for all those who are able. The main beneficiaries of the SPP were the poor living below the absolute poverty line and the unemployed, and more specifically, members of the under-privileged and less advantaged groups particularly exposed to poverty.

The Enhanced Productivity Program (EPP) was created in 2002 to take the approach further, aiming to improve the standard of living for all Jordanians, especially rural and disadvantaged individuals, by creating and increasing access to opportunities for productivity gains in each of the governorates.

The decision to launch EPP developed from consultations between the public, private, and non-governmental sectors, and the consensus that was reached on national socio-economic priorities during the Second National Economic Forum in March 2001. The EPP is a government-funded development project for Jordan. Unlike previous government initiatives, the EPP focuses on an integrated approach to rural development where one EPP project leads directly to, and supports another. The end result will be individuals and communities generating income and employment in their towns and villages, with the government playing the role of enabler and supporter.

Jordan now has 15 international, governmental and non-governmental organizations sponsoring around 14,000 income-generating projects for women, the disabled, the unemployed and underprivileged individuals, as well as for Palestinian refugees.

Prominent among these organizations is the Development and Generating Fund (DGF) which enables needy individuals and households to engage in work and production by extending soft loans of up to JD 10,000 (US$ 14,000) to help them set up small-scale projects that would contribute to further job opportunities and alleviate the severity of poverty. The DGF also gives loans indirectly through the Queen Alia Fund and the Agricultural Credit Corporation. The National Aid Fund has also financed over 6000 income-generating projects, the loans from which will be repaid over a period of ten years with no interest.

However, though such schemes operate in a number of countries, they tend to be on a very limited scale.

Big Society

There are other initiatives aimed at raising the profile of 'social' issues. David Cameron, the UK Prime Minister, in 2011 raised the notion of the 'Big Society' – a society in which citizens collectively take responsibility for 'social well-being'. Though the concept was derided by many as a means of lowering expectations about future social service funding, the introduction of the concept did act as a means of raising the level of debate about the way in which future social services were to be delivered and funded.

When we move to the organisational level, too few business organisations are asking questions such as … "What kind of business practices can begin driving shared value and improved social outcomes?"

Social Enterprises

There are example of what are termed 'social enterprises' – organisations that have an explicit social mission and trade solely to fulfil that mission. Though such organisations may be charities, they seek to raise funds by trading goods and/or services rather than by seeking donations.

Some of these could be termed 'self-help social enterprises'; others operate to a fairly standard business model but have strong social aims. Importantly, both kinds of enterprise are quite distinct from traditional charities.

27

Yunus (2009) makes this distinction clear.

A social business is not a charity. It is a business in every sense. It has to recover its full costs while achieving its social objectives. When you are running a business you think differently and work differently than when you are running a charity. And this makes all the difference in defining social business and it's impact on society.

One well-known – and successful – social enterprise from the UK is The Big Issue. The Big Issue is a magazine launched in 1991 by Gordon Roddick and A. John Bird in response to the growing number of rough sleepers on the streets of London. The two set out to address the problem of homelessness by offering homeless people the opportunity to earn a legitimate income – by selling the magazine - thereby 'helping them to help themselves'. Created as a business solution to a social problem The Big Issue has gone on to become an instantly recognisable brand in the UK.

In 2012, the organisation was working with around 2800 homeless and vulnerably housed people across the UK, and circulating over 125,000 copies of the magazine every week. Selling the Big Issue releases vendors from a dependence on charitable or social welfare hand-outs and provides an alternative to begging.

Impressive as some of these organisations might be, they are outside of the mainstream of business. It is only when such a social focus comes into the mainstream that significant and sustainable change is likely to occur.

Luckily there are exemplars 'out there'. Most people can cite a small number of examples of business organisations that are addressing social issues alongside environmental issues … and it is very often the more successful companies (in terms of their economic productivity) that adopt such a stance.

In January 2012, RBC - a large, Canadian bank employing over 70,000 people - announced a $20 million commitment to a new social and environmental initiative aimed at facilitating solutions to social and environmental problems. "Impact finance" describes a range of financial vehicles and services that use private capital to finance solutions to social and environmental challenges while generating financial return, and is expected to help drive the next wave of innovation and productivity growth in the global economy.

This initiative is comprised of:

• A new $10 million capital fund - the RBC Impact Fund - to help finance projects by organizations and entrepreneurs tackling social and environmental challenges. Priority areas will include projects promoting environmental sustainability and water resource management, and providing employment opportunities for youth and newcomers to Canada; and

• A $10 million investment by the RBC Foundation of its own assets into Socially Responsible Investment (SRI) funds.

Social Enterprises Supporting Social Enterprise

There is also a third variety of social enterprise where a business, operating on a profit-making business seeks to provide support services either wholly or significantly to existing social enterprises or services. Plum Pie Media, for example, is an organisation operating in South Yorkshire in the UK, providing professional video, design and marketing services. They specialise in working with social enterprises and third sector organisations (but also businesses) to provide "high quality, engaging, creative, affordable services". They use their profits to work with schools, youth centres and community groups to enhance the curriculum, engage disenfranchised young people and raise the profile of community issues.

29

Changing Business Models

These examples are laudable and exemplary but certainly do not represent the business mainstream. It is only when some of this thinking reaches that mainstream that real change will occur.

In Chapter 1 we suggested that social productivity (as part of wider SEE productivity) should be regarded as a business issue, not a philanthropic add-on.

Let's look at an example of this in practice. 'Big Pharma' (the generally derogatory term for the large pharmaceutical companies) have been urged to donate drugs to causes like the treatment of HIV/Aids – with people suggesting that they use a share of their vast profits to 'do some good'. Whilst this approach has superficial attractiveness, such 'generosity' must, by definition, be limited … and is unlikely to solve the problem of the difficulty of making expensive drug treatments available to relatively poor communities.

One of the companies, Novartis, realised that this approach was not going to be successful and chose to adopt a different approach entirely. They decided to review the way that certain drugs were packaged, marketed and distributed to see if savings could be made and passed on to consumers. Now this is a real productivity approach – changing the 'value' paradigm of the product – looking at the top and bottom lines of the productivity ratio but doing so through a 'social' as well as an 'economic' lens.

What Novartis did was to create a different business model (or, perhaps more accurately, to refine an existing business model) which was capable of growing the market, contributing to the societal problem under consideration but doing so in a way that was self-sustaining for Novartis.

This seems to confirm the research we looked at in Chapter 1 that seems to show that addressing these factors is good for business but makes the important point that organisations have to 'think through' these issues as 'business issues' and identify changed approaches to the way things are done that enable 'win-win' progress to be made.

Reporting

Tell it like it is!

Increasingly, commercial organisations are reporting on their efforts to address environmental and social concerns. A report from KPMG on their *International Survey of Corporate Responsibility Reporting* in November 2011 suggested that 95% of the world's 250 largest companies reported on their environmental and social performance, up from 80% in 2008.

Interestingly, though – in line with the general not-quite-mainstream status of CSR - the major drivers for such reporting were reputation and brand status (two thirds of companies) and ethical considerations for just under 60 per cent.

Reporting Standards

The leading model for preparing sustainability reports is offered by the Amsterdam-based Global Reporting Initiative. The guidelines for the GRI cover a variety of environmental performance indicators, relating to the 'big issues' of water usage, energy consumption, greenhouse gas emissions, and waste handling. There are also 'social issues' relating to the labour force, injury statistics and equality/discrimination factors.

The GRI suggests that over 1,800 companies worldwide prepared reports using the GRI framework in 2010, up 22 percent from 2009 – a good improvement but a remarkably small percentage of the total number of companies.

SEDEX

Sedex, the Supplier Ethical Data Exchange, is a not for profit membership organisation which aims to help members improve the application of responsible and ethical business practices in their global supply chains.

Interestingly, Sedex HAS recognised the powerful link between those responsible and ethical practices and business performance, suggesting that joining Sedex can help an organisation to:

- drive improvements in ethical and responsible business practices
- increase efficiency
- save time and resources
- improve supplier engagement
- boost productivity
- reduce reputational risk
- gain competitive advantage
- help drive collaboration and reduce duplication

Though Sedex does not offer a specific standard, it does help organisations to audit their own practices in relation to 'ethical trade'.

Ethical Trading Initiative

The Ethical Trading Initiative is an alliance of companies, trade unions and voluntary organisations working in partnership to "improve the working lives of poor and vulnerable people across the globe who make or grow consumer goods - everything from tea to T-shirts, from flowers to footballs".

The 'base code' of the ETI – the minimum standards of practise that they promote are that:

1. Employment is freely chosen

1.1 There is no forced, bonded or involuntary prison labour.

1.2 Workers are not required to lodge "deposits" or their identity papers with their employer and are free to leave their employer after reasonable notice.

2. Freedom of association and the right to collective bargaining are respected

2.1 Workers, without distinction, have the right to join or form trade unions of their own choosing and to bargain collectively.

2.2 The employer adopts an open attitude towards the activities of trade unions and their organisational activities.

2.3 Workers representatives are not discriminated against and have access to carry out their representative functions in the workplace.

2.4 Where the right to freedom of association and collective bargaining is restricted under law, the employer facilitates, and does not hinder, the development of parallel means for independent and free association and bargaining.

3. Working conditions are safe and hygienic

3.1 A safe and hygienic working environment shall be provided, bearing in mind the prevailing knowledge of the industry and of any specific hazards. Adequate steps shall be taken to prevent accidents and injury to health arising out of, associated with, or occurring in the course of work, by minimising, so far as is reasonably practicable, the causes of hazards inherent in the working environment.

3.2 Workers shall receive regular and recorded health and safety training, and such training shall be repeated for new or reassigned workers.

3.3 Access to clean toilet facilities and to potable water, and, if appropriate, sanitary facilities for food storage shall be provided.

3.4 Accommodation, where provided, shall be clean, safe, and meet the basic needs of the workers.

3.5 The company observing the code shall assign responsibility for health and safety to a senior management representative.

4. Child labour shall not be used

4.1 There shall be no new recruitment of child labour.

4.2 Companies shall develop or participate in and contribute to policies and programmes which provide for the transition of any child found to be performing child labour to enable her or him to attend and remain in quality education until no longer a child; "child" and "child labour" being defined in the appendices.

4.3 Children and young persons under 18 shall not be employed at night or in hazardous conditions.

4.4 These policies and procedures shall conform to the provisions of the relevant ILO standards.

5. Living wages are paid

5.1 Wages and benefits paid for a standard working week meet, at a minimum, national legal standards or industry benchmark standards, whichever is higher. In any event wages should always be enough to meet basic needs and to provide some discretionary income.

5.2 All workers shall be provided with written and understandable information about their employment conditions in respect to wages before they enter employment and about the particulars of their wages for the pay period concerned each time that they are paid.

5.3 Deductions from wages as a disciplinary measure shall not be permitted nor shall any deductions from wages not provided for by national law be permitted without the expressed permission of the worker concerned. All disciplinary measures should be recorded.

6. Working hours are not excessive

6.1 Working hours comply with national laws and benchmark industry standards, whichever affords greater protection.

6.2 In any event, workers shall not on a regular basis be required to work in excess of 48 hours per week and shall be provided with at least one day off for every 7 day period on average. Overtime shall be voluntary, shall not exceed 12 hours per week, shall not be demanded on a regular basis and shall always be compensated at a premium rate.

7. No discrimination is practised

7.1 There is no discrimination in hiring, compensation, access to training, promotion, termination or retirement based on race, caste, national origin, religion, age, disability, gender, marital status, sexual orientation, union membership or political affiliation.

8. Regular employment is provided

8.1 To every extent possible, work performed must be on the basis of recognised employment relationship established through national law and practice.

8.2 Obligations to employees under labour or social security laws and regulations arising from the regular employment relationship shall not be avoided through the use of labour-only contracting, subcontracting, or home-working arrangements, or through apprenticeship schemes where there is no real intent to impart skills or provide regular employment, nor shall any such obligations be avoided through the excessive use of fixed-term contracts of employment.

9. No harsh or inhumane treatment is allowed

9.1 Physical abuse or discipline, the threat of physical abuse, sexual or other harassment and verbal abuse or other forms of intimidation shall be prohibited.

Social Accountability International

SAI is a non-governmental, multi-stakeholder organization whose mission is to advance the human rights of workers around the world. It partners to advance the human rights of workers and to eliminate sweatshops by promoting ethical working conditions, labour rights, corporate social responsibility and social dialogue. SAI established one of the world's pre-eminent social standards—the SA8000 standard for decent work, a tool for implementing international labour standards – and, recognising that voluntary codes of practise often need some form of 'disciplinary agency' provides training and certification services. (The 'standards' in the SA8000 are similar to those in the ETI base code.)

Increasingly, this proliferation of information, guidance, codes of conduct and 'good practice' is leading to governments shaping legislation that forces companies to report on some of these (especially environmental) issues.

For example,

- South Africa began requiring companies listed on the Johannesburg Stock Exchange to submit annual sustainability reports in 2003.
- Denmark started requiring large companies to list policies related to the environment as well as human rights and other societal concerns in their annual financial reports in January 2009.

Where such government 'encouragement' does not exist, it is investors and investor groups (who use sustainability reports to judge the degree to which companies are addressing current and future risks) that are driving the introduction of such reporting. Investors have also shown increasing interest in transparency along the supply chain and companies are responding to this 'pressure' by mandating levels of performance or reporting for members of that supply chain.

Microsoft, for example, announced in October 2011 in response to a shareholder proposal, that it would start requiring suppliers to report on their compliance with the company's environmental protection, labour, human rights, and other standards in 2013

Measuring Progress and Success

There are organisations and agencies looking at, and trying to measure, whether there are performance and benefits in addressing these issues.

Jantzi Research Inc. is an independent investment research firm, founded in 1992 by Michael Jantzi, that evaluates and monitors the environment, social and governance performance of securities.

The Jantzi Social Index is a Canadian stock market index created in 2000 with the purpose being to measure the effect of a socially and environmentally conscious stock market index on market behaviour.

The Jantzi Social Index is a market capitalization-weighted common stock index consisting of 60 Canadian companies that pass a set of broadly-based social and environmental screens.

The index was created as a benchmark against which money managers and other investors can measure the performance of socially screened portfolios ... by comparing the performance of these companies to a 'control set' on the Toronto stock exchange.

Over the period the index has existed there have been ups and downs (as with any measure linked to stock prices) but the Jantzi index has compared very favourably to the underlying market.

Working Through the Supply Chain

We refer above to large companies mandating reporting on environmental (and occasionally social) performance by members of their supply chain.

This 'influence' also extends to encouragement, and sometimes even support, by leading performers amongst those large companies, to members of their supply chain to:

• Improve their environmental performance
• Comply with specific third-party standards
• Meet specific levels of performance.

The UK supermarket chain ASDA (part of the Wal-Mart group), for example, has launched an online hub, in partnership with the sustainable business community 2degrees, to help their suppliers to improve their performance in relation to water, energy and waste.

The hub, part of ASDA's Sustainability 2.0 strategy, is known as the Sustain & Save Exchange and sets specific targets for ASDA's products and for its supply chain. The exchange provides opportunities for suppliers to share information ask questions and identify opportunities for collaboration and, as this book was being written, was being piloted amongst 70 fresh food suppliers before being rolled out across the complete supply chain.

Local Social

At a more local level, many firms seek to address their social responsibilities by interacting in some positive way with local communities. Such interaction could be via schemes such as:

- Secondments of staff (full or part-time) to work on a specific task with a local, community organisation
- Schemes under which staff can volunteer, out of working hours, on an individual or a team basis to offer a particular skill set or contribute to a particular community aim
- Offering work experience to member of the local community – youngsters about to leave school or perhaps the long-term unemployed.
- Employee fundraising where the organisation 'adopts' one or more local charities and encourages staff to engage in fundraising activities

A specific example is that of the Shell Geelong refinery in Australia which, as part of a wider social and environmental programme, has committed to providing assistance to not-for-profit organisations that are seeking funding for projects beneficial to the local community.

The Shell Employee Community Grants Committee has been established to consider grant applications with an education focus or objective which will benefit Geelong's northern suburbs community.

The Committee calls for submissions twice yearly (usually in February and September) and assesses applications according to a set of criteria and guidelines. The maximum amount an organisation can apply for is $5000 (per round).

So, there is good work going on – but on the fringes of business, highlighted by its relative rarity … and more often related to environmental rather than social, productivity.

It also seems as though there is quite a number of companies that are 'signed up' but not necessarily 'geared up' to deliver on their commitment.

Technology Support

In Chapter 1, we talked about the way in which technology changes things – makes things possible which were once impossible … and creates new opportunities for the 'little guys' to take on the 'big guys'. This, of course, is true in all arenas – and so, must be true in the field of social productivity.

In addition to the ways in which technology can help any organisation (and therefore any organisation with a social conscience) – by improving communication, by automating operational processes, etc - one of the ways in which technology can help is to assist the 'concerned citizens' we have talked about to exert their influence on commercial organisations and on politicians … to show that they exist not only as interested stakeholders, but – more importantly – as powerful, interested stakeholders.

41

This process has become known as Digital Engagement and uses technology for two main aims – fundraising and advocacy … raising money and 'making a fuss'. For example, it is relatively easy for organisations to create petitions, to lobby politicians, to write to the media, to organise protest marches and so on.

This enables relatively small organisations to have a relatively large voice (and this is not the place to debate the degree to which that should be so in a democratic society!).

However, we will see more in the future. What we are seeing at the moment could possibly be more accurately labelled Digital Engagement 1.0 and we will surely move towards Digital Engagement 2.0 as these stakeholders realise the power of the technology that, as yet, lies relatively unexploited.

One such example is Kiva (www.kiva.org), a web-based, non-profit organization with a mission to connect people through lending to alleviate poverty. Working through a worldwide network of microfinance institutions, Kiva lets individuals lend as little as $25 to entrepreneurs (most often in developing countries) who do not have access to standard banking facilities. One hundred percent of any loan is sent to one or more of the microfinance institutions, which Kiva terms 'Field Partners', who administer the loans in the field.

Kiva relies on a world wide network of over 450 volunteers who work with these Field Partners to edit and translate borrower stories, and ensure the smooth operation of a range of other Kiva programs.

The technology that enables Kiva to work has been around for a number of years (and, in fact, Kiva has been around since 2005) but the imagination of individuals and groups is only just catching up. Partly, perhaps, because exploiting technology means such organisations have to invest quite heavily in 'backroom systems' and, naturally, their preferred course of action is to direct all their money to front-line services. We will, in the future, see more organisations understand this relationship between infrastructure and service and start to exploit technology to improve social productivity.

Why is there not more happening?

In the 2010 review of the UN Global Compact, Georg Kell, the Executive Director, commented on why good intentions do not always translate into effective actions.

(The Global Compact is a strategic policy initiative for businesses that are committed to aligning their operations and strategies with ten universally accepted principles in the areas of human rights, labour, environment and anti-corruption. Remember, though that the companies who have signed up to the Compact – the ones Georg is talking about - have taken the step of engagement, by signing. They are thus a self-selecting set of committed organisations.)

Georg suggests that:

• Though CEO awareness and commitment is high, execution and implementation is low.
• Execution might be effective within corporate headquarters but often does not spread to operating divisions, and certainly not to the supply chain
• There is not sufficient adoption of appropriate measures to drive improving performance.

Stimulating further thought and action

We suggested at the start of this Chapter that 'social productivity' was not just an issue for developing countries – and we cited the increasing income differentials in western, developed countries as evidence. Yet, this Chapter has shown us that most of the standards, codes of practice and reporting frameworks are clearly aimed at those operating in developing countries. There is still much work to do!

The Institute of Productivity aims to stimulate further thought and action in relation to social productivity … and in particular aims to demonstrate the business case for addressing SEE productivity as a balanced, improvement programme.

One of the ways in which we intend to do this is to show governments, aid funders, NGOs, charities and responsible business organisations how they can assess the impact of potential SEE development projects before they are implemented.

For 'social' projects, for example, we aim to help 'investors' to assess likely payback in terms of both financial and social impact.

The second book in this "Getting It Done" series is "Measuring Social Impact for Policies, Programmes and Projects: Getting It Done" and takes the reader through current thinking and then through a practical guide on measuring such impact.

References

Cheetham, S. (2008)
Corporate social responsibility: philosophy to practice, fruition or
failure?
MBA Dissertation, University of Huddersfield

Commission on 2020 Public Services (UK) (2010)
Final Report: From social security to social productivity: a vision for
2020 Public Services

OECD (2011)
Divided We Stand: Why Inequality Keeps Rising

Prahalad, C.K. (2004)
The Fortune at the Bottom of the Pyramid: Eradicating Poverty
through Profits
Wharton School Publishing

Yunis, M. (2009)
Creating a World Without Poverty: Social Business and the Future of
Capitalism
PublicAffairs

3 The importance (and problems) of measurement

Governments make policy. Government policies are a statement of intent for how they wish to shape the future of their country. The policy might be based on a fundamental political viewpoint but will also be dependent on an assessment of the current 'state of the nation' and the government's declared priorities for 'improvement'.

The generic (and simplified) cycle of policy development can be represented by:

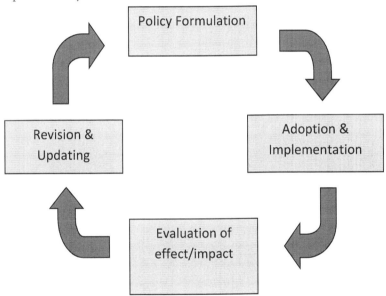

Clearly without the third stage ("Evaluation of effect/impact"), a government has no evidence against which to judge the success/failure of the policy and no basis on which to refine, update and improve the policy. Measurement is the means by which we provide information for evaluation.

Similarly, organisations make plans. They may have a sophisticated strategic planning process which informs tactical and then operational planning ... or they might have a relatively informal operational plan and schedule. In either case, they need to know whether the plan is working ... they need to know how they are performing ... they need to know if the plan needs to be modified. They find this out by measuring (or assessing) their actual progress/performance against the planned (or expected) progress/performance. Where there is a difference (and especially where actual progress/performance is behind that of the plan), they can then take some corrective action ... or at least understand the reasons for a lack of progress and adjust plans and expectations accordingly.

Even (or especially?) in the case of a government, there may be no formal 'plan' ... but the policy is a statement of intent, a commitment to change, and will almost certainly have some indicators of how that change will manifest itself ... a reduction in child poverty, an increase in the take-up of tertiary education or whatever.

This (perhaps vague) 'picture of the future' is the equivalent of our organisation's more fully-formed 'target'. Both our government and our organisation need to measure or assess progress in order to judge how well they are doing and whether they are 'on track'.

So, measurement of progress and performance is a key element of control.

Measuring the Money

Measuring productivity can be a relatively simple matter – or a rather complex one. As with most measurement, it depends on what you want to do with the measures – and therefore how important is:

- Level of detail
- Accuracy
- Reliability

The OECD, for example, devotes a 150 page manual to the topic of "Measuring Productivity: Measurement of Aggregate and Industry-level Productivity Growth". (OECD 2001) However, if we simply want the ability to compare/benchmark one country with another on a high-level aggregated measure of economic productivity, such data is readily available in a simple format – for example, measures of GDP/capita or GDP/hour worked.

Similarly, many organisations have whole reporting and control regimes based around the measurement of actual and planned performance according to the annual budget (and its monthly or weekly breakdown).

However, in most industries, production/service cycles are shorter than they used to be, and the pace of change and innovation is faster. This makes the retrospective reporting that most budgetary control systems involve completely inadequate. By the time the organisation knows it is 'out of budget' because it has failed to control its costs, the market has moved on.

So we need a 'better' set of measures; measures that provide control and correction information fast enough to be useful.

The rise of the Balanced Scorecard over recent years is testament to the fact that many organisations have realised that they need to measure more than financial matters – if they are to get a 'balanced' view of how well they are doing. (See Footnote on The Balanced Scorecard at the end of this chapter.)

The measures an organisation adopts must reflect their specific plans and priorities.

If we think – as we set out in Chapter 1 – that to be truly sustainable and viable in the longer term, we have to address social, environmental AND economic productivities, then we have to include measures that address each of these dimensions of our performance.

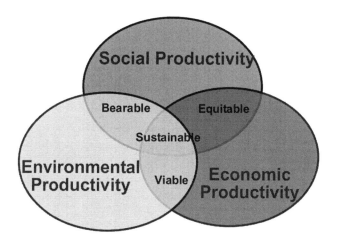

Measuring our financial performance is certainly not enough. It is not even enough to give a full view of 'economic performance' since as we hint above it tends to be a reasonable indicator of past performance ... but not of future performance. So whatever form of measurement regime and process we use, our 'scorecard' must address social, environmental and economic measures.

The same is true at national level. In Chapter 1 we discussed an increasing trend for the 'judges' of performance – concerned citizens, environmental activists, NGOs, and so on – to base judgment on this wider set of criteria (involving social, environmental and economic productivities). Both our organisation and our government have to be informed by, and respond to, this change in perception and judgement.

There is a growing consensus that environmental performance and climate change will be financially significant to all companies (Collin, 2009) and that investors will increasingly take into account environmental, social and governance (ESG) issues when making financial investments in companies (United Nations Principles for Responsible Investment).

Many businessmen have already realised that environmental performance is part of company performance … and should be 'sold' as such.

For example, when talking about investment products, the United Nations Environment Programme suggests that if a product is labelled 'ethical' or 'SRI' (a sustainable and responsible investment), it will appeal only to a narrow range of investors. If the positive financial characteristics of a product (e.g. in terms of risk-adjusted return, diversification, etc.) are highlighted, then the potential range of interested clients increases. (United Nations Environment Programme)

These businessmen are also realising that positive value and negative value can both result from environmental impact. The CSR (corporate social responsibility) 'movement' is a manifestation of this realisation (though oddly enough in the light of the title, most CSR programmes focus on environmental rather than social factors).

So, we have to set about building a set of performance measures or performance indicators that gives us an overall, balanced view of how well we are doing across our complete set of plans and priorities.

Of course the nature of measurement will be significantly different at national level than at organisational level.

At national level, just as when we adopt aggregated economic performance measures (such as GDP/capita or per hour worked) we need to identify and use appropriate high-level, aggregated measures for social and environmental performance.

At the organisational level, some of the measures and indicators will be macro measures … the kind of measures an executive team might receive on a weekly or monthly basis to judge the overall performance of the organisation. One problem of such macro measures is that they are summary measures; they are presented periodically. Yet they represent the totality of the performance on lots of lower level actions that were necessary to complete the process or activity being measured. If we 'leave it here' we face the danger that when the senior team look at these measures, they realise something is wrong … but it is too late to take corrective action. The process, batch or order is complete – complete with errors, mistakes, delays, scrap or whatever.

We, clearly, cannot allow this to happen. So, these 'high level' measures need to be 'translated' into lower level measures so that we can find out whether things are going wrong within a timeframe that allows us to do something about it.

We might measure production volumes in real time – with automatic counting of output as it leaves the machine. We might have batch quality checks at regular intervals to identify whether parts made are within the agreed quality specification. Such measures also apply to 'production' in offices, hospitals, shops and other types of workplace.

Key and Critical Performance Indicators

What we try to do is build an overall measurement regime that keeps us in control.

Though we might measure lots of things, there is usually a small number of really important things to be measured – the things we must measure to ensure that we are doing the right things – and doing them right. These are the key performance indicators.

Some of these will relate to longer-term, strategic issues. Some, however, will relate to (perhaps very) short-term issues where we need to know what the measure is so we can take corrective action before we make faulty goods, use unnecessary resources, cause pollution or whatever.

These measures are the 'critical performance indicators ... the kinds of things that the CEO might ask about on a daily or weekly basis.

Both key and critical performance indicators measure performance on critical success factors - the things the organisation must do, and must do well, if it is to achieve its overall mission – but they do so over different time and control scales.

> Critical success factors are the things we have to **do, and do right,** if we are to be successful.
>
> Key and critical performance indicators tell us whether we are getting our critical success factors right.

Lagging and Leading Indicators

One categorisation of performance indicators is into 'lagging' and 'leading' indicators. Lagging indicators are measures taken at the end of a process or cycle; they tell you what performance was ... but offer no chance of changing that performance. They may well be 'key' performance indicators that show performance on important factors but they simply give you the historical record.

Leading indicators, on the other hand, are measures taken in-process and reflect current (or sometimes even future) performance. Leading indicators are much more likely to be critical performance indicators in that they may offer the chance to take corrective action and change performance.

On first thought, it seems that critical performance indicators are more important and should be 'indicators of choice'. However they can be more difficult to build and use and they do not always give a complete picture.

In the environmental field, the use of lagging indicators may be mandated by regulatory authorities; organisations might, for example, have to report annually on their performance in relation to specific toxic wastes. Lagging indicators also have the advantage that they are often readily quantifiable and understandable, and the data are often collected for other business purposes.

Most measurement regimes therefore contain a mix of leading and lagging indicators – of 'key' and 'critical' performance indicators.

Defining Success

Each organisation must identify a small number of these factors that 'have a significant impact on success' ... and that move the organisation forward towards the organisation's overall aims in support of the mission.

One useful approach is to start with the 'voice of the customer', then think about the views of other stakeholders, what your competitors are (or might be) doing, the changes that are occurring outside of your control (regulatory change, technological change, etc) and then come up with your critical success factors (CSFs) ... those things that you have to do - and have to do right – to succeed and grow.

To help identify CSFs, we should ask:

What is it that we do that if we stopped doing the organisation would die?

What would hurt us most if it went wrong?

What is it that we must do if we are to grow?

What do we want to have happen in this time period if we can concentrate on only a few things?

Though this discussion has related to organisations, the principles remain the same at government policy level. In fact, government policy-setting is, in effect, the identification of the critical success factors – those items against which the government seeks to be judged. The 'pictures of the future' we referred to earlier are the definitions of success for these policies.

Once we have identified our 'success', we need to know how well we are doing in relation to these factors ... and whether we are getting better or worse over time?

The success factors must be translated into key and/or critical performance indicators ... those things the organisation (or the government) should measure to know it is 'on track', that it is getting the things done that result in the critical success factors looking good!.

As we have suggested, for an organisation, these will exist at a number of levels as the 'top level' indicators (representing the whole organisation or a complete process) are translated into 'tactical' indicators (perhaps representing a specific product, a specific division or department, a specific sub-process) and into 'operational' indicators (perhaps representing a specific machine, a specific workgroup, or a specific point-of-sale).

The whole (practical) process of identifying, developing and using critical performance indicators is tackled in a companion book "Managing Using Key & Critical Performance Indicators and Associated Benchmarks: Getting It Done". For now, we are going to look at some of the principles, especially in terms of addressing our SEE productivity factors.

If we are committed to improving all of the SEE productivities, we need performance measures or indicators that relate to all of these.

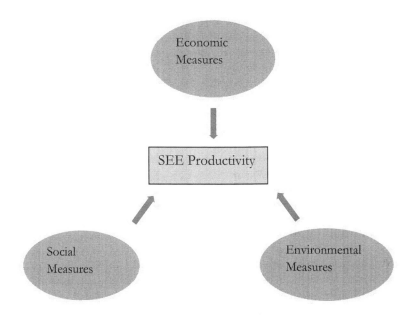

Any measurement or assessment regime for SEE productivity (like all effective measurement regimes) should:

• Provide information in a timely fashion, within the 'time span of discretion' of those able to influence SEE activities

• Provide a balanced view so that subsequent improvement actions are not sub-optimal

• Present information clearly and concisely so that the underlying messages are themselves clear

• Involve the use of measures that are deemed credible by both those being measured and by those using the measures as a means of decision-making

• Be cost effective

Can social and environmental issues be measured?

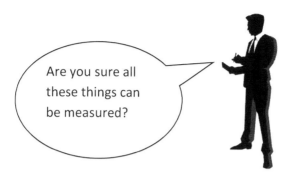

Are you sure all these things can be measured?

Can the same tools or the same concepts that determine the economic wisdom of a 'standard' business decision (building a new plant, launching a new product) be appropriate when making environmental decisions?

One side of the debate suggest they are …. or perhaps that they must be if businesses are going to take note of social and environmental factors in complex decisions.

The other side asks how you would measure, for example, the 'value' of a reed warbler being around in 50 years in a particular location.

As in many such situations, the answer probably lies somewhere in the middle. There are social and environmental factors that can be measured and accounted for. And there are many current, 'standard' business decisions that include an element of 'faith', recognising that not all can be measured … but we can still put value on it … good design, for example. This reflects back to the CSR (Corporate Social Responsibility) and ESG (Environmental, Social, Governance) concepts: in effect, good practice in these areas adds value to the overall company 'brand'.

We seem to have taken some time to arrive at where we are – but it is important to recognise two simple 'truths':

- all of social, environmental and economic measurement is a fundamental component of the control and improvement processes
- nations and organisations will increasingly be judged on their performance against all of these productivities

In the next couple of chapters, we are going to see how we set about creating measurement regimes for nations and organisations … in terms of creating control and improving performance, we will establish ways of "Getting It Done!"

Footnote: The Balanced Scorecard

The Balanced Scorecard (BS) is a conceptual framework that attempts to overcome the limits of many performance measurement/management approaches that rely entirely on financial measures.

BS attempts to translate an organization's vision and mission into a set of performance indicators and was originally set around four perspectives:

- Financial (If we are to achieve our vision and mission, how should we appear to our shareholders and investors?)

- Customer (If we are to achieve our vision and mission, how should we appear to our customers?)

- Internal Business Processes (If we are to satisfy our shareholders and customers, what business processes do we need to excel at?), and

- Learning and Growth (How can we create and sustain an ability to change and improve?)

Thus, the scorecard provides an enterprise view of an organization's overall performance by integrating financial measures with other key performance indicators.

The Learning & Growth perspective is considered important since it reflects potential future performance - it directs attention to the basis of all future success - the organization's people and infrastructure. Adequate investment in these areas is critical to all long term success.

The Internal perspective focuses attention on the performance of the key internal processes which drive the business. Obviously, the nature of the processes are dependent on the nature of the organisation - the scorecard is not a 'fully-cooked' solution, it must be tempered and tailored to meet the specific circumstances of each organisation.

In order to translate effective internal processes into organisational success, customers/clients must be happy with the service they receive. The Customer perspective considers the business through the eyes of the customers, measuring and reflecting upon customer satisfaction.

Finally, the Financial perspective measures the results that the organisation delivers to its stakeholders. Together, these four perspectives provide a balanced view of the present and future performance of the business.

The aim of this measurement process is to direct, and help manage, change in support of longer-term strategy - and to manage, rather than simply measure, performance.

Though this was the shape of the original scorecard, a number of organizations take the overall concept but use their own 'dimensions' based on their own strategic priorities.

The concept was introduced by Professor Robert Kaplan and Dr. David Norton in 1992, and has since been adopted by a wide range of organisations around the globe. It is well-represented in the business press, having been the subject of a best-selling book (see below) and numerable articles in prestigious journals.

If used properly, the Balanced Scorecard becomes a catalyst for change. The performance measurement is not an end in itself - nor should the measurement be reified; it simply serves to illustrate, to diagnose, to aid analysis. 'Accuracy' is therefore not essential - but confidence in the measures as true indicators is.

The Scorecard must become integrated into the strategic planning of the organisation - as a tool for identifying pressure points, conflicting interests, objective setting, prioritisation, planning and budgeting.

It is often associated with a 'dashboard' – a graphical means of presenting performance data to managers which ensures that all the elements present in the balance can be viewed and considered at the same time.

The BS – and the means by which the data are presented - together offer managers a comprehensive, **balanced** view of their organisation – based on their own priorities - upon which they can make strong decisions and upon which they can base real change.

References

Collin, S
The Value of Environmental, Social and Governance Factors for Foundation Investments
EIRIS Foundation Charity Project, May 2009

Kaplan,R.S. and Norton, D.P.
The Balanced Scorecard: measures that drive performance
Harvard Business Review, vol 70, issue ,1992

OECD 2001
Measuring Productivity: Measurement of Aggregate and Industry-level Productivity Growth
OECD Publications, France

United Nations Environment Programme
Unlocking Value: The scope for environmental, social and governance issues in private banking
http://www.unglobalcompact.org/docs/issues_doc/Financial_markets/Unlocking_Value_.pdf
(accessed 13th Dec 2009)

4 Measurement at national level

We have chosen to address separately issues of measurement at the national and the organisational level. This does not, of course, mean that SEE productivity at the national level is in any way different from SEE productivity at the organisational level. Clearly as with standard economic performance, it is the contribution of thousands of organisations that make up performance at a national level.

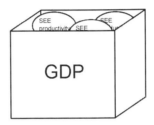

Where we are differentiating is in the process – and problems of – measurement.

We have established that it is going to be increasingly important for nations to address their social, environmental AND economic performance ... and that in order to do this they will need measures of each of these factors.

The other factor to be borne in mind is that governments need to be able to benchmark themselves against other nations – to identify their level of competitiveness. At the national (and organisational) level, productivity is a competitive factor; what matters is our level of productivity in comparison to our main competitors.

This means, of course, that when measuring social, environmental and economic productivity, we need a consistent set of measures that will allow such comparisons to be made.

For economic productivity, this is not a problem. For many years, nations have compared their economic performance using the simple (but generally effective) measure of GDP/capita.

This is, of course, not the only – or even the best - measure of economic performance but it does have the advantages of simplicity and therefore relative consistency.

Alternative measures may attempt to be more specific, and/or more sophisticated. An alternative measure is that of competitiveness – having the advantage that, a bit like productivity, it is a better predictor of future economic performance than a simple measure of current economic performance.

For example, the World Economic Forum's Centre for Global Competitiveness and Performance through its Global Competitiveness Report series, aims to mirror the business operating environment and competitiveness of over 140 economies worldwide.

The GCI uses 140 indicators to rank countries according to twelve competitiveness pillars. The impact each pillar has on the competitiveness ranking depends on the country's stage of development, which is decided according to the economy's reliance on: factors (unskilled labor, natural resources); efficiency (higher product quality and improved production process); innovation (ability to compete with new and unique products).

Let us take a look at an example – that of Pakistan

Pakistan is currently classified as a factor-driven economy, meaning that emphasis is placed on the indicators related to institutions, infrastructure, health and primary education, and macroeconomic stability

The pillars on which the competitiveness ranking are measured are: institutions, infrastructure, macroeconomic environment, health and primary education, higher education and training, goods market efficiency, labour market efficiency, financial market development, technological readiness, market size, business sophistication and innovation.

.Despite many challenges, Pakistan's ranking in the Global Competitiveness Report 2011-2012 improved by 5 places. Pakistan was been ranked in 118th position, against 123rd position the previous year.

Critical areas of improvement were largely related to human resources and institutions. Other areas in which ranking has improved are financial market development, market size and business sophistication.

Pakistan continues to exhibit strong competitive advantages in innovation and sophistication while facing ongoing challenges in many of the more fundamental and factor-driven indicators. Pakistan's ranking for innovation (Pillar 11) and business sophistication (Pillar 12) continued to improve

However, Pakistan ranks below 100th place on 7 of the pillars. These include institutions, infrastructure, macroeconomic environment, health and primary education, higher education and training, labor market efficiency, and technological readiness. (Thanks to Neelam Dawood of the National Productivity Organisation, Pakistan for the analysis.)

The advantage of looking at these scores is not that they tell you precisely where Pakistan stands, but that they do indicate Pakistan's relative strengths and weaknesses and can be used by the government and NGOs to target development activity. This is particularly important for the National Productivity Organisation of Pakistan who, with limited resources, need to focus their attention on where it might do most good.

Similarly, the Pakistan Institute of Trade & Development can use the data to help analyse those business processes which seem to be hindering Pakistan's export competitiveness and can start, with the help of the private sector, to target specific infrastructure issues that should 'make a difference'. The aim is not to 'chase the rankings' but to make changes which do positively affect competitiveness – and should be reflected in future series of the GCI.

For social and environmental productivity, the issue is not so straight forward. There are numerous factors that could be measured that could be said to represent (some aspect of) environmental performance; and there are also measures that can be said to reflect the outcomes of social productivity. However, our awareness of the factors involved in both these arenas changes relatively quickly and thus appropriate measures need to be revised.

'Modern' interest in measuring sustainability was rekindled following the 1992 United Nations Conference on Environment and Development in Rio de Janeiro.

One of the conclusions to emerge was that:

Indicators of sustainable development need to be developed to provide solid bases for decision-making at all levels and to contribute to a self-regulating sustainability of integrated environment and development systems.

In terms of social factors, perhaps the best-known measurement exercise has been that of the Human Development Index pioneered by the U.N. Development Programme. The first *Human Development Report* in 1990 opened with a simple premise:

People are the real wealth of a nation.

If we are to 'exploit' the potential of people and convert that 'wealth' of resource into other forms of wealth, we have to ensure those people live longer and healthier, and are well-educated and well-trained.

(Note that this is a true win-win situation: the people get a better quality of life and the nation gets a more valuable resource (thereby increasing its productivity).

The UN has used this basic concept to derive a set of data and construct an index of 'human development'.

(http://hdr.undp.org/en/statistics/hdi/)

A number of attempts have been made to construct multi-faceted indices, in effect alternative models of measurement to replace or augment GDP as the main means of assessing a nation's performance and growth. One of these is the Genuine Progress Indicator, itself a variant of the Index of Sustainable Economic Welfare proposed by Daly and Cobb (1989). Interestingly unlike most progress on such measures in recent times, the GPI mitigates GDP with social, rather than environmental factors.

In 2006, Talberth, Cobb and Slattery provided an update on the GPI. They describe the way in which GPI, and similar measures, are calculated starting with estimates of personal consumption expenditures, weighted by an index of the inequality in the distribution of income to reflect the social costs of inequality and diminishing returns to income received by the wealthy. Additions are made to account for the non-market benefits associated with volunteer time, housework, parenting, and other socially productive time uses as well as services from both household capital and public infrastructure. Deductions are then made to account for purely defensive expenditures such as pollution related costs or the costs of automobile accidents as well as costs that reflect the undesirable side effects of economic progress. What such measures show for most countries is a widening gap between a measure of the country's and a measure of one of these modified figures. This suggests a lessening, over time, of the impact of GDP growth on improved welfare and well-being.

However, though data is available for the GPI for a number of countries, it has never established itself as a universally-accepted measure – perhaps because of the problems of identifying reliable, comparable data.

Since the World Confederation of Productivity Science believes that the concept of SEE, and its measurement, is so important, it decided to set about creating – from first principles - a simple index of SEE productivity (combining the social, environmental and economic factors) that could be used for inter-nation comparisons.

As the President of WCPS, John Heap presented a very early model for a SEE index at the World Productivity Congress in Turkey in 2010. Since then he has worked with a colleague, Tom Burgess (Leeds University Business School and a Fellow of the World Academy of Productivity Science) to refine the concept and build a simple and up to date, but robust and rigorous, social, environmental and economic (SEE) index that supports progress towards sustainability.

Obviously it was necessary to build an index that stood up to 'academic' scrutiny and therefore was based on some kind of established and credible process. After some research and thought, we decided to adopt a methodology taken from an OECD Handbook (2008) which describes how a composite indicator can be formed by combining a number of individual indicators into a single index on the basis of an underlying model. We have used this methodology to combine measures of national social, environmental and economic performance into a single, composite SEE index.

The OECD Handbook suggests a ten-step guide to building a composite index (or indicator):

1. Theoretical framework
2. Data selection
3. Imputation of missing data
4. Multivariate analysis
5. Normalisation
6. Weighting and aggregation
7. Robustness and sensitivity analysis
8. Back to the detail
9. Links to other indicators
10. Visualisation of the results

These ten steps have been used to construct the SEE Index

As mentioned earlier, 'adopting' an established and accepted measure for national economic productivity was not difficult. We selected the most common (and readily-available) measure of national productivity, GDP per capita.

Though environmental productivity is a little more problematical (in that there are many facets and factors involved, depending on the industrial sector(s) being considered), we thought that it was (relatively) safe to adopt a measure that has been the subject of much international discussion (and negotiation) in recent years – that of 'carbon emissions' and so to represent environmental performance we chose a measure of metric tonnes of CO_2 produced per capita per year.

A measure of social performance proved more problematical since it is a relatively new concept. (Hopefully Chapter 2 has helped you understand what we in the Institute of Productivity mean by social productivity.)

In developing countries, social productivity is a measure of the degree to which a nation invests effort (and part of its generated wealth) into such things as:

- reducing poverty
- increasing employment levels
- improving hygiene and health
- improving participation in education
- increasing educational success rates
- reducing corruption
- reducing crime

Of course this means that we knew we were unlikely to find a set of existing data which could act as a 'proxy' for social productivity – and we thus had to start thinking of measures which could reflect components of social productivity and could be combined into a single measure.

We also thought that some of the items on this list (reducing poverty, increasing employment levels) – though they have social implications – could more properly be considered as economic factors.

Our research into 'social factors' led us to the constituents of the UN Human Development Index referred to earlier which combines living standards (i.e. economic), health and education indices.

The latter index combines two measures (i) mean years of schooling for adults aged 25 years and (ii) expected years of schooling for children of school-going age, to provide a measure of educational progress in the country.

Because our proposed overall SEE index already had an economic component, the economic element of the UN HDI was discounted and a social index formed by combining the factors that make up the health and education indices; i.e. life expectancy and the two educational components (see Figure 4-1).

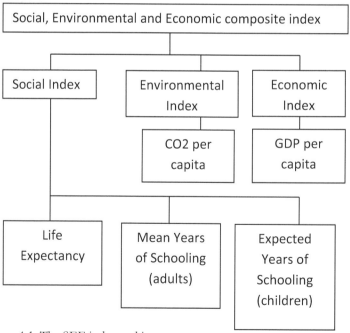

Figure 4-1: The SEE index and its components

Data Sources

It would not have been possible for us to collect data on these measures for ourselves, so we needed an existing, authoritative and reliable data source. (Of course the factors we chose to use were partly chosen because such data sources were known to exist.)

We selected the UN website as our main source of data (though Table 4-1 shows all constituent variables and their sources of data). When we first built the index (in early 2011) the latest data available for CO_2 emissions was from 2009 while the other data series were available for 2010. To use a consistent base year across all measures, data for 2009 were taken as the base for all the variables.

The OECD methodology is a series of processes for dealing with missing data, undertaking multivariate analysis, normalising the data and carrying out sensitivity analysis. These processes are relatively complex and are therefore omitted from this book, but the full process of constructing the SEE index is detailed in the paper by Burgess and Heap (2012).

Table 4-1: Constituent variables and data sources

Component	Constituent Variables	Source
Social	Life expectancy at birth	United Nations Statistics Division http://unstats.un.org/unsd/default.htm
	Mean years of schooling (adult)	UN (as above)
	Expected years of schooling (children)	UN (as above)
Environ-mental	Metric tonnes of CO_2 per capita per year	US Energy Information Administration http://www.eia.gov/
Economic	Gross domestic product (US dollars at current prices) per capita per year	UN (as above)
Population	Country population in millions	UN (as above)

The SEE Index

So, what does it show us?

Using the OECD methodology, an index was created, based on 2009 data, for 194 countries (although there are some limited areas where data were missing).

The resulting index is one that embraces the heart of the debate around this area, namely that a country's environmental performance appears to trade-off against performance in the economic and social realms.

Not surprisingly perhaps, the index suggests that high economic performance for a country facilitates high performance on the social component (i.e. high GDP per capita leads to high investment in social infrastructure such as health care and schooling) but comes at the cost of a high carbon footprint.

A number of "small" countries (in terms of population size) appear near the top of the SEE index. These small countries are not generally significant in terms of the global position and we chose therefore to categorise countries by size and concentrate on the larger countries. However we should point out that that all the indices, i.e. the overall SEE index and the three components, are uncorrelated with population size. In general, high and low performing countries appear at all sizes of countries. However, size does have some impact since the overall SEE index for the world when country values are weighted by population is 0.90; this suggests that, in general, large countries are lower performing than smaller ones.

When the countries are organised in descending population size then 35 countries are above the mean and together these countries comprise 81.4% of the world population. (See Table 3-2)

Though there are 'expected' factors in the rankings (the index is dominated by the wealthy, well-developed economies), there are some surprises which show that a SEE index does indeed measure differently than a 'simple' economic index.

We need to measure this index over time to identify whether policy decisions taken now (on alternative forms of energy supply, on waste reduction and recycling, and so on) do, in fact, have the intended effects in terms of enhancing performance – in this more rounded look at the concept of productivity.

Of course any one nation needs to understand how its performance measures up against other nations – and, in particular, against nations at the same broad level of economic development.

This benchmarking of performance is an important aspect of measurement and of assessment – and the theme of benchmarking is taken up elsewhere in this series of books.

Table 3-2: SEE Index and population for 35 largest countries

Country	Population (millions)	Population Rank	SEE index	SEE Rank for 35 largest countries	SEE Rank for all 194 countries
China	1347.6	1	0.795	26	136
India	1241.5	2	0.671	30	158
United States	313.1	3	1.341	7	31
Indonesia	242.3	4	0.938	18	110
Brazil	196.7	5	1.219	10	53
Pakistan	176.7	6	0.655	31	160
Nigeria	162.5	7	0.720	27	148
Bangladesh	150.5	8	0.681	29	154
Russian Federation	142.8	9	0.841	22	125
Japan	126.5	10	1.646	1	8
Mexico	114.8	11	1.163	12	58
Philippines	94.9	12	1.094	15	73
Viet Nam	88.8	13	0.834	23	126
Ethiopia	84.7	14	0.504	35	184
Egypt	82.5	15	0.830	24	128
Germany	82.2	16	1.507	5	17
Iran	74.8	17	0.842	21	124
Turkey	73.6	18	1.039	16	82
Thailand	69.5	19	0.893	20	118
Congo (Dem. Rep)	67.8	20	1.146	14	64
France	63.1	21	1.619	2	9
United Kingdom	62.4	22	1.536	6	21
Italy	60.8	23	1.536	3	13
South Africa	50.5	24	0.698	28	151
Korea (Rep of)	48.4	25	1.311	8	37

Table 3-2 continued

Country	Population (millions)	Population Rank	SEE index	SEE Rank for 35 largest countries	SEE Rank for all 194 countries
Myanmar	48.2	26	0.621	33	167
Colombia	46.9	27	1.185	11	55
Spain	46.5	28	1.533	4	14
Tanzania	46.2	29	0.593	34	171
Ukraine	45.2	39	0.914	19	115
Sudan	44.6	31	0.632	32	166
Kenya	41.6	32	0.804	25	134
Argentina	40.8	33	1.221	9	52
Poland	38.3	34	1.159	13	59
Algeria	36.0	35	0.965	17	102

Perhaps it is clearer to show the 'Top 10' based on economic performance only (Table 3-3)... and then how they look when we consider the SEE index (remembering that these are based on 2009 figures ... when we update the index, things may have changed somewhat in the light of the economic recession).

Table 3-3 Top 10 Economic Rankings with their SEE Ranking

Country	Economic Ranking	SEE Ranking
USA	1	7
Germany	2	5
UK	3	6
France	4	2
Japan	5	1
South Korea	6	8
Spain	7	4
Italy	8	3
Poland	9	13
Argentina	10	9

The fact that 9 of the Top 10 economic performers are also in the Top 10 of SEE rankings seems to suggest that economic performance is a key underpinning of SEE performance …. but equally the changes in rankings also seems to show that some aspects of economic performance are 'at odds with' a more rounded assessment of performance.

Though this SEE index can clearly be refined, for now, we do have a composite measure – of SEE productivity – that can be used to:

- compare national performance levels
- stimulate further debate about these important issues
- serve as a means of measuring the impact of social and environmental policies

However, this is not enough. The title of this book refers not only to measurement but to improvement. Governments also need to know how to influence the SEE measure so that they can improve their productivity and their ranking. This involves addressing all of the SEE factors – social, environmental and economic productivity. It might mean addressing – and improving them individually … but, of course, a government – like a commercial organisation – has to understand the 'trade-offs' between the factors … to understand when improving economic productivity might hinder environmental productivity, for example.

In fact this is a time when it is useful for governments to learn from (the best) commercial entities. They need to undertake a similar exercise that we are going to take organisations through in the next few chapters – starting with an understanding – and a clarification – of their priorities (their policies) … and their success factors. For most governments this will be a mix of economic and other factors – with those other factors relating to issues such as law and order, health, education, etc … and perhaps to environmental factors.

This means that governments have a single, simple measure of their 'global' SEE performance and (once they have worked through the Getting It Done section) can also establish a measurement regime for the key factors that they believe shape their particular SEE strategy.

They can then know whether, when they attempt to move forward taking a balanced approach to development; whether they are in fact Getting It Done!

References

Burgess, T.F. & Heap, J.P. (2012)
Creating a sustainable national index for social, environmental and economic productivity
International Journal of Performance & Productivity Management, vol 61, issue 4.

Daly, H. and Cobb, J. (1989)
For the Common Good: Redirecting the Economy Toward Community, the Environment, and a Sustainable Future.
Beacon Press.

Handbook on constructing composite indicators: Methodology and user guide (2008). Organisation for Economic Co-operation and Development.

Talberth, J., Cobb, C., and Slattery, N.(2006)
The Genuine Progress Indicator 2006: A Tool for Sustainable Development
Redefining Progress. Oakland, CA, USA

5 Measuring at the organisational level

Like nations, organisations want to measure their performance on the SEE factors so that they:

- have a balanced view of their performance
- identify their level of competitiveness
- can identify areas where they might improve their performance
- build long-term sustainability

Again, this means they need consistent measures that will allow them to compare and benchmark against their chosen competitor base.

Of course, in this sometimes cynical world, companies sometimes simply want to show off their 'good guy' credentials in relation to the SEE factors, without being saddled with the burden of measurement … or more likely by just using a carefully selected sub-set of measures that make them look 'good'.

But, let's not be cynical. There are, fortunately enough 'real good guys' around to show that the 'movement' is a true movement towards greater awareness of sustainability and the factors involved.

What are organisations doing to improve their SEE productivity?

The economic crisis of 2009-10 has led a number of governments and organisations to question some of the business practices that have been rife over the last couple of decades. Many firms seem to have been trading in traded options, almost 'inventing money' using circuitous, far-from-transparent chains of transactions. In Chapter 2, we saw that this realisation of the extent of this trading in 'virtual value' had led to calls for change – some even suggesting that the concept of capitalism itself needs to be reviewed. There is still recognition that capitalism remains one of the best systems under which wealth can be created ... but now people are looking at:

- The need to redefine terms such as 'value' and 'wealth' in the context of social and environmental issues. What is the point of a government building the infrastructure to support enhanced productivity if the majority of citizens are not going to benefit when that productivity is realised?

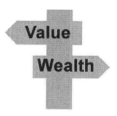

- The need to distribute that (redefined) wealth more equitably across a wider range of stakeholder groups.

We, of course, tend to think in productivity terms – in terms of ratios of outputs to inputs. When we look at social productivity, we focus on 'the top line', on building more value into an organisation … but we also look at value over a longer-term period (as one must when trying to build sustainable business models). In fact, this is one of the great strengths of SEE productivity; it makes an organisation take a longer view. We saw in Chapter 3 that the kinds of measures and indicators we use for social issues are key performance indicators, but rarely critical performance indicators in terms of the timescale of monitoring and review.

In Chapter 2 we gave a couple of examples of organisations engaging in social productivity and we have repeatedly asserted that more companies are engaged in improving their environmental productivity. Do we have evidence of this?

Well, Harvard Business School's "Working Knowledge' of January 2012 reported that over 1,000 business leaders participate in *We Can Lead*, a coalition that calls for the passage of comprehensive climate legislation. Similarly, 20 large consumer companies such as ice cream producer Ben and Jerry's and Aspen Skiing Company are members of Business for Innovative Climate & Energy Policy (BICEP), a leading advocacy group calling for bipartisan climate legislation.

Some organisations make a 'big thing' about their programme addressing environmental and/or social issues, recognising that it can be an important factor in improving brand value. (It is almost always beneficial in business terms to be seen as one of the 'good guys'.) Some take this one stage further and actually brand their sustainability or CSR programme itself … and promote this brand aggressively. Marks & Spencer, the large UK retail chain, for example have a comprehensive programme aimed at improving their environmental performance. Various aims and targets associated with this programme are displayed boldly in their stores so that customers cannot escape some awareness of what Marks & Spencer call "Plan A" (because there is no Plan B).

For now let us assume that many businesses are concerned with measuring their SEE performance for the right reasons. They do, however, have a problem. For organisations, selecting appropriate measures is more difficult. For example, when we selected a measure to represent environmental productivity at the national level, we chose a highly aggregated measure of carbon emissions.

Though organisations have to understand their own 'big picture', they also need to be able to control operations at the detailed, micro level.

Secondly, in some sectors there are indicators of different significance because of the nature of the business. Some sectors might have unique measures and indicators. For example in the paper-making industry, water consumption might best reflect the impact an organisation has on the earth's natural resources; in other sectors a more appropriate indicator might relate to energy consumption, effect on air quality or levels of effluent produced .... or indeed some combination of measures.

Each sector has its own particular set of products and services. Within that sector each organisation has its own organisation structure, financial structure, legal and regulatory requirements, customer demands, data collection and management systems ... and its own environmental impacts.

So, potential measures might relate to:

- Discharge of agreed priority pollutants
- Electricity/gas consumption
- Solid waste management
- Amount of hazardous waste generated
- Percentage of water retreated and reused
- Change in land use/land cover

For social productivity, we also have an additional problem. Any business has two main areas of social impact – the impact it has on its own employees and the impact it has on the communities in which it operates (recognising, of course, that these overlap since employees will normally come from those surrounding communities).

Those (global) companies that address BIG social productivity (especially in developing countries) might measure the impact their operations have on the access by their workforce or the local community to water, sanitation, education and credit.

Those looking more internally (and in more developed countries) might look at issues such as skills development amongst the workforce or the engagement of the workforce in decision-making.

Somewhere in the middle we have factors such as engagement of the workforce in charitable projects within the local community, donations to local causes, etc.

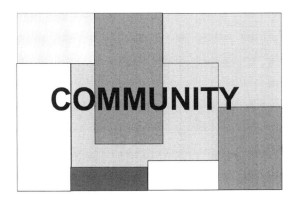

All of these can be measured in some way, of course, though, as we suggested earlier, measures in these areas are likely to be key performance indicators, rather than critical performance indicators since they change slowly and need relatively infrequent review.

Financial (economic) productivity is less of a problem. There is a raft of measures commonly used to reflect financial performance and agreed conventions for creating and reporting on such measures.

Since we do not want too many measures in our set of measures (too confusing and distracting) we have to prioritise the 'critical performance indicators' – those that give early warning of 'out of control' situations and those that maximise the opportunities to make improvements.

One advantage of starting with financial performance is that financial measures often help us in determining our performance on the other SEE factors – and especially environmental productivity. (Less so in regard to social productivity since social factors often do not impinge directly on operational costs; they do, however, impinge on longer-term financial well-being. This is one of the failings of any 'operational' analysis – it might miss factors involved in the 'big picture' that have longer-term and higher level effects. Social factors might emerge from the strategic planning process rather than from the operational control processes.)

So, we come at the 'problem' from two different directions – and in so doing we are much more likely to identify the full range of factors we should be addressing.

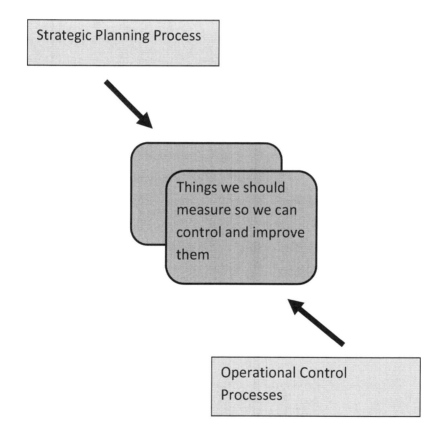

What we end up with is a set of key performance indicators – important but high level, strategic and longer-term, and another set (or sub-set) of critical performance indicators, again important but this time probably lower level, and shorter-term. These critical indicators need more prompt and careful management. Because of our commitment to longer-term sustainability, these indicators will cover all of social, environmental and economic productivities.

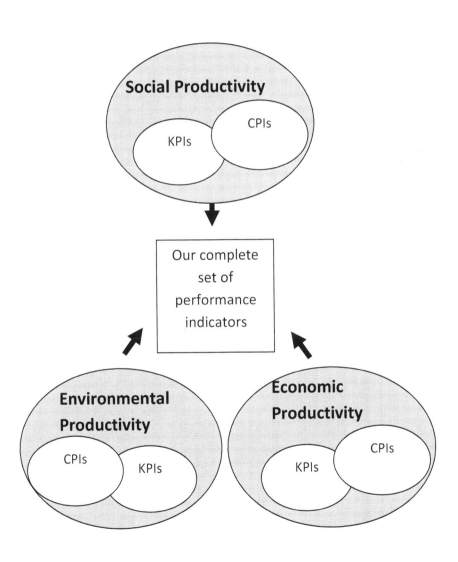

Of course, some performance indicators might relate to one or more of the SEE factors. Energy consumption, for example, is both an environmental and an economic factor.

In practice, indicators relating to social productivity (and some of those relating to environmental productivity) are less likely to be 'critical' indicators, not because they are less important but because they tend to operate over longer-time scales. So, if we measure the training and development activity of our workforce, or the donations (of money, materials and/or time) we make to the local community, or the amount of waste going to landfill … these are important to our longer-term development and sustainability, but are unlikely to change often or on a weekly basis. Thus we will monitor them but perhaps on, say, a quarterly basis. They are not the kind of indicators the CEO wants on his/her desk every Monday morning.

Of course, some companies are 'ahead of the curve' in relation to measuring SEE productivity (though as we have already commented, such measures are much more likely to relate to environmental – rather than social – productivity.

We will take a look at a couple of examples to show:

- The kinds of commitment some business organisations are making to measurement of these factors
- The types of measures they are using to drive improvement.

Puma's Environmental Profit & Loss Account

Puma (the sports and leisure group best known for its sports footwear) in 2011 became the first company to publish a specific profit & loss (P&L) account relating to environmental issues. This is particularly important – to publish a P&L requires robust measurement.

The sports and leisure group reported that the combined cost of the carbon it (and its suppliers) emitted and water it used in 2010 was 94.4m euros ($134.3m; £82.8m).

Puma said that reducing its environmental impact would improve its future performance and that the figures would help it to build a more "resilient and sustainable business model", and prepare for potential future environmental taxes.

> "The business implications of failing to address nature in decision making are clear - since ecosystem services are vital to the performance of most companies, integrating the true cost for these services in the future could have significant impacts on corporate bottom lines."

Puma enlisted the help of consultancy firm PricewaterhouseCoopers (PwC) and environmental research group Trucost to calculate the impact of its business on the environment.

They found the impact of greenhouse gases was equivalent to 47m euros, while that of water use was 47.4m euros.

Interestingly, the company's suppliers made up the majority of this total - more than 37m euros.

As a result of the environmental profit and loss calculations, Puma said it would ensure that outsourced processes such as embroidering and printing would be subject to the same environmental and social standards as its own manufacturing processes.

The company set a target of reducing its carbon, waste, energy and water use by 25% by 2015.

Toshiba' Measurement of Eco-Efficiency

Toshiba is another example of a company attempting to measure the impact of its business on the environment. It has developed a process built around the concept of 'Factor T', an eco-efficiency indicator used to assess a product's value in relation to its environmental impact over its life cycle. The higher the product value in economic terms or the lower the life-cycle environmental impact, the greater is the eco efficiency. (The 'T' in 'Factor T' stands for nothing more imaginative than 'Toshiba'.)

$$\text{So eco-efficiency} = \frac{\text{Product Value}}{\text{Environmental Impact}}$$

Toshiba uses the QFD (Quality Function Deployment) technique as a method to express a product value.

QFD is a process by which real customer requirements are determined based on actual opinions obtained from customers and set against design specifications in a matrix to assess the degree to which the specification of the product meets - or does not meet - those customer requirements. (Toshiba Social and Environmental Activities)

Lean manufacturing includes the concept of 'critical to customer' (CTC) and 'critical to quality' (CTQ) factors. CTCs are those things that the customer regards as important – and is willing to pay for. They are 'deal breakers' in a customer buying decision. CTQs are those aspects of the manufacturing process that ensure the delivery of CTCs. QFD in effect is a matrix-based evaluation of the links between these CTC and CTQ factors. (iSixSigma)

Toshiba uses this QFD technique to calculate the product value of Factor T, while non dimensional numeric values are determined depending on important Engineering Metrics by comparing the quality between the benchmark product and a product subject to assessment, so that the numeric values can be integrated as product value indicator (value factor).

Environmental impact is calculated using "Easy-LCA"- a simplified evaluation tool for life cycle assessment (LCA) developed by Toshiba in 1996, which incorporates an environmental impact database based on the Input-Output Tables serving as statistics of the inter-industry shipment value in Japan, which is able to calculate 30 types of environmental loads (inventory) in the life cycle. Essentially this involves assessing the consumption of energy and materials, and emissions into the air and into water.

Perhaps the most important aspect of this process is that it brings in to the equation the value placed on a product by the customer – after all, this is the only real measure of 'value'.

This is, ironically, both a simple and a sophisticated measurement process. Sophisticated in the sense that Toshiba has 'thought through' what is important to them … yet simple in the sense that it uses relatively easily-available data to create the measures used.

In 2010, Del Monte foods reviewed and refined its environmental goals, setting specific targets to be achieved by 2016 in three key areas: waste reduction, greenhouse gas emissions and water usage. The targets are set against performance in 2007 as the base year so that improvement can be clearly and transparently established.

Del Monte is working to:

- lower the amount of waste going to landfill by 75%
- reduce packaging materials by 15%
- reduce manufacturing and distribution greenhouse gas emissions per ton of finished product by 10%
- reduce water usage by 20%

Lessons

Two important lessons emerge from these examples.

1. The environmental impact of an organisation's business activities can not be measured by simply measuring the direct impact of the organisation's own activity. There may, as in the case of Puma, be significantly more impact generated by the activities of other companies in the supply chain.

2. The environmental impact of a product is not only the impact created during the manufacturing and distribution process. Further impact is created during its use over its lifetime and, often especially, by the process of disposal at the end of its life.

Each organisation must determine its own priorities and them identify appropriate measures which show progress towards targets representing those priorities.

Puma's Environmental P&L is part of a wider move by companies to look at what is called integrated reporting, which looks to incorporate the cost and benefits of environmental and social impacts into financial accounts … partly because they have to respond to the demands of investors who are beginning to realise that the sustainability agenda impacts on financial returns.

As natural resources (water, fossil fuels, etc) become ever-more scarce, businesses will have to pay to protect them or, in some cases, replace them. In fact, in many cases they will be forced to pay, for example by regulatory instruments such as pollution taxes and higher insurance premiums.

Qualitative Measures

So far we have concentrated on trying to put 'numbers' onto our measures. But, of course, we have chosen to use the word 'indicator' to represent the things we are assessing – and not all indicators are quantitative. Hard-headed businessmen generally prefer to work with numbers - but we need to recognise that sometimes we might have to deal with non-quantifiable (or certainly less quantifiable) factors.

One common approach is to 'translate' qualitative judgments into quantitative figures – to allow easier comparison. This is fine as long as we recognise that we are dealing with assessments and indicators and not 'proper' measures.

The same is true of factors that will contribute to the measures but for which it is difficult to assign a direct contribution. For example, we might expect that allowing our staff to participate in team volunteering (and perhaps even donating some of the employees' time) might contribute to lower levels of staff turnover.

If we measure staff turnover 'down the line', it might have improved – but it would be difficult to assign a direct, quantifiable, causal relationship back to the volunteering.

This, of course, is a job for business leaders. They often have to take decisions based on an 'act of faith' (I believe that if we do X, it will benefit the company in the following ways). Certainly what they must not do is to ignore factors that cannot be – directly – measured or they are likely to miss opportunities to contribute (significantly) to performance figures in the longer-term. (This is the reason that people – hopefully – read books like this; they are sure it will benefit their future performance in some way, but it will be impossible to measure the ways in which that improvement actually happened.)

In practice, the distinction between quantitative and qualitative data is perhaps too polarised. An executive taking a decision based on accurate, robust quantitative data might be basing his/her decision on a (qualitative) judgement about the effects of the factor being measured on the situation under review.

So, we should accept both forms of data and use them as the basis of appropriate indicators of performance and productivity ... .and we should accept the limitations and constraints of both forms of data.

In the specific case of volunteering, the Deloitte Volunteer IMPACT research series has focused for a number of years on measuring important aspects of corporate community involvement. (Deloitte, 2012)

The 2011 survey suggests that those who frequently participate in workplace volunteer activities are more likely to be proud, loyal and satisfied employees, as compared to those who rarely or never volunteer. These and other findings suggest a link between volunteerism and several drivers of employee perceptions of positive corporate culture. One can infer a link between volunteering through proud, loyal and satisfied employees to employee engagement and an impact on the bottom line… but one cannot measure it directly.

Those companies addressing environmental productivity now are taking action to reduce their environmental impact and the associated costs, and are doing so because they believe they can gain a competitive advantage. Similarly the smaller number of companies measuring their social productivity now is taking action to increase their social impact and is again often doing so because they believe they can gain a competitive advantage.

Each organization – based on its particular context and its particular priorities, has to consider whether it want to adopt a particular standard or benchmark – for all or part of its operations. This clarifies the data collection process and makes inter-firm comparison easier … but any particular standard (or set of standards) might not give the specific 'balance' necessary to meet an organization's own set of priorities.

What we are trying to do – in this book – is to find ways of helping you to create measures that build your assessment of performance against those elements of the SEE agenda that matter to you.

In Chapter 7 we will take you through the practical steps involved in working through this process … Getting It Done!

References

Deloitte (2012)
Volunteerism
http://www.deloitte.com/view/en_US/us/About/Community-Involvement/volunteerism/index.htm
(accessed Jan 2012)

ISixSigma
http://www.isixsigma.com/dictionary/Critical_To_Quality_-_CTQ-216.htm
(accessed Jan 2010)

Toshiba Social and Environmental Activities
http://www.toshiba.co.jp/env/en/products/ecp/factor.htm
(accessed Dec 2009)

6 Benchmarking

We mentioned earlier that it is helpful to adopt measures that are comparable with those used by other (similar) organisations so that we can compare our performance and have a better indication of whether we are performing 'well" or 'badly'. This process of comparison is known as 'benchmarking'.

We can adopt:

- 'internal' benchmarking – where we compare the performance of one of our processes or departments or divisions against the performance of a similar process, department or division

For example, if we compare levels of absenteeism across a number of departments, and we find there are some excellent performers, we might be able to go further and identify the practices that are leading to this high performance …. and spread it throughout the organisation or

- 'external' benchmarking - where we compare our performance against the same kind of unit in a different, but similar, organisation … and, especially, where we compare our performance to that of an organisation that is regarded as an exemplar, as 'best in class'.

Of course, 'external' might mean international … but we then have to be more careful about the analysis of reasons underlying performance differences as there may be a wider range of factors involved – including, for example, different regulatory regimes and different cultural factors.

(Internal benchmarking is clearly of little use if we do not feel there is existing good practice in the area under study in at least a part of our organisation!)

The aim is to compare performance and, if possible, to compare structures, processes, procedures, relationships, levels of investment, etc so that we know the level and nature of resources that our comparator organisation is using to achieve their level of performance. This (which is much more like a productivity measure) gives us a much more robust comparison than if we only look at 'output' levels.

Alongside this, another aim is to motivate people within our organisation (or part of it) to strive to achieve those same high standards.

The aim is not to 'copy' the benchmark organisations, but to learn from them and to adopt and adapt elements of their organisation only as far as they can fit within our own structure, culture and broad strategy. Thus benchmarking is often a component of a wider improvement process such as business process re-engineering or quality improvement.

Simply attempting to analyse what makes a good company good - even when that company is in another industry - is a useful exercise. (See "Good to Great" by Jim Collins – Random House in which the author compares firms in the same sector which he identifies as either 'good' companies or 'great' companies and then tries to identify what makes the difference.)

Of course, it is important to do more than simply compare the data and find out that your performance looks 'good' or 'bad'. It is the analysis of 'why' that results in improvement.

One advantage of benchmarking is that it helps with the setting of 'realistic' targets - after all, if another organisation has achieved them, they must be realistic. It also helps us be aspirational – by looking at other organisations we can decide between targets which indicate mere competence and those that indicate a degree of excellence.

So how do we get data to use as the basis of benchmarking? Well, information which is freely available in the public domain can be useful as a starting point, but the level of detail is probably inappropriate for really effective benchmarking analysis. Thus, the usual approach is to share data with another organisation (or group of organisations) - on a mutual help basis. There is now a number of benchmarking 'clubs' both within and across certain industry sectors where members collectively pool data - derived to a common measurement methodology - to act as collective benchmarks for the group. (This data is often aggregated and anonymous as many organisations do not want their individual performance in specific areas or on specific processes to be common knowledge.)

It is important to choose the right organisations to benchmark against - they should be clearly the same kind of organisation (or, if not, we should be aware of the differences and their effect on benchmarked activities). It is equally important to identify the right activities to benchmark - those that align with our strategic aims and objectives … those where we have identified appropriate performance measures and indicators.

It is usually best to benchmark against some sub-set of a total system so that causes and effects can be more easily identified and followed. A complete system can thus be addressed in phases with each process being benchmarked and improved in turn.

Benchmarking agencies and clubs

In Chapter 2 we referred to a number of 'standards' and 'guidance documents' relating to 'social issues' – though with a caveat that many of these are aimed at organisations operating in developing countries. These might be a 'first consideration' for benchmarks –as some of them have well-established processes of support, development and audit that can help organisations think through the issues involved.

A 'next port of call' is the Trade Association – they are sometimes helpful in organising and sharing benchmark data across a specific sector or sub-sector.

For example, PWC operate a 'Global Best Practices knowledge base' which offers a number of quantitative benchmarking tools to help a company analyse its process performance relating to:

- Accounts payable

- Accounts receivable

- Close the books

- Finance & accounting

- Finance effectiveness

- Human resources

- Information technology

- Insurance consolidation and reporting

- Internal audit

- Inventory management

- Payroll

- Purchasing

- Supply Chain

- Tax

In the UK the Local Authority Performance Benchmarking Club provides members of the Club with a set of Excel based tools which contain comparative information on key performance measures both for outturn performance at the end of each year, and also quarterly in-year data.

The tools enable easy analysis of the data and presentation in simple to read graphs, to show for example:

- comparative performance in relation to upper, mid and lower quartile on individual indicators or across service groups;
- year on year improvement in Council performance; and
- relative performance improvement from one year to the next, showing one Council's rate of improvement compared to others.

The objective is to use the tools to both raise awareness amongst officers and Councillors of the Council's performance, and to help identify any areas which require targeted attention.

If no such data is available, you may need to join one of the 'clubs' and (unfortunately) this might cost you a 'membership fee'.

One of the 'big players' is AQPC (it seems to prefer this relatively anonymous title rather than its former title of the American Productivity & Quality Center).

In 1991 the APQC set up the International Benchmarking Clearinghouse, offering a wide range of benchmarking services across almost all industrial and commercial sectors. In 2004 APQC launched the Open Standards Benchmarking Collaborative to create the first common (global) database of process definitions, surveys, and measures, enabling organizations to benchmark their performance.

Similarly, there are organisations and agencies working in the 'corporate social responsibility space' that can offer advice on identifying and measuring environmental and social factors … and some of these can provide benchmark data.

For example, Business in The Community (BiTC) is a UK-based organisation that has established a CSR index and offers a range of support and services, including benchmarking, diagnosis and management tools. (See www.bitc.org.uk)

The CSR index is designed to allow participating organisations to:

• Benchmark their CSR performance against their sector peers and against 'best practice' organisations from across the index

• Undertake a gap analysis of areas where future progress could be made

• Track their progress as they move to upgrade their performance and their place on the index

In addition, companies who participate publicly, making up the annual CSR Index ranking, demonstrate a commitment to transparently improving their social and environmental impacts and further benefit from public recognition of their commitment.

The ARENA Network in Northern Ireland has conducted the annual Northern Ireland Environmental Management Survey since 1998.

This business led initiative is widely recognised as the principal measure of environmental engagement in Northern Ireland and examines the leading 200 companies, government departments, local councils, Health Trusts and the education sector.

The Survey benchmarks organisations against both their sector peers and the leading Northern Ireland organisations, on the basis of their environmental management and performance in key areas.

A voluntary exercise, the Survey is intended to help organisations analyse gaps, measure progress, drive improvement and raise awareness of environment performance as a strategic, competitive issue at board level.

In 2011, 128 organisations from 15 different sectors took part, reaching an average score of 68% - not an important figure in itself but one with which participating organisations can compare their own performance.

So, to summarise, we benchmark for the same sorts of reasons that we measure in the first place. Benchmarking:

- provides realistic and achievable targets

- stops us from being complacent (when we think our performance is 'good' but we do not know that our competitors' performance is 'better')

- gives us something to aim for in our continuous improvement

- allows employees to see what is possible – providing a strong motivator for change

- helps to identify areas where we are weak … and indicates what might be achieved if we improve.

SECTION 2

GETTING IT DONE!

.

Section 2: Prologue

Though some of the terminology and some of the factors under discussion will be different, we hope that the preceding chapters have made you realise that the steps involved in Getting It Done apply at both national and organisation level. Both governments and organisations are trying to establish a set of measures which they can use to assess their performance against their own aspirations and against that of their competitors. They will use different measures, different sets of benchmarks, different standards and so on – but the principles remain the same. We use the term 'regulatory factors' to suggest that commercial organisations may have to comply with the law and with specific regulation; this also applies to governments. Governments may have 'higher' levels of government over them - think European countries subject to laws and regulations created by the European Parliament - and they may be party to self-imposed 'regulation' as part of international environmental treaties.

Throughout these next chapters, rather than try and cover all bases, we will use language that assumes the reader is from a commercial organization. This means that government representatives will have to 'translate' the processes we take you through into appropriate language and context for their activities.

7 Establishing measurement factors

OK. We've gone through the (important) background stuff you need to know. It is now time to talk you through the process of 'getting it done' … of establishing a process where you measure what you need to measure in order to get to where you plan to be.

We are going to assume that you know 'where you plan to be' … that you have your strategic plans in place … if not, as a formal written plan, at least as an agreed and shared 'vision' of where the organisation in heading.

If that doesn't apply, you do really need to do that first. We suspect that if you are reading this book, that you are planners and preparers and that you can 'tick off' this part of the process.

If you do know where you plan to be, Figure 7.1 shows – in outline – what you have to do.

Figure 7.1 outline of the GID process for establishing measures of SEE productivity

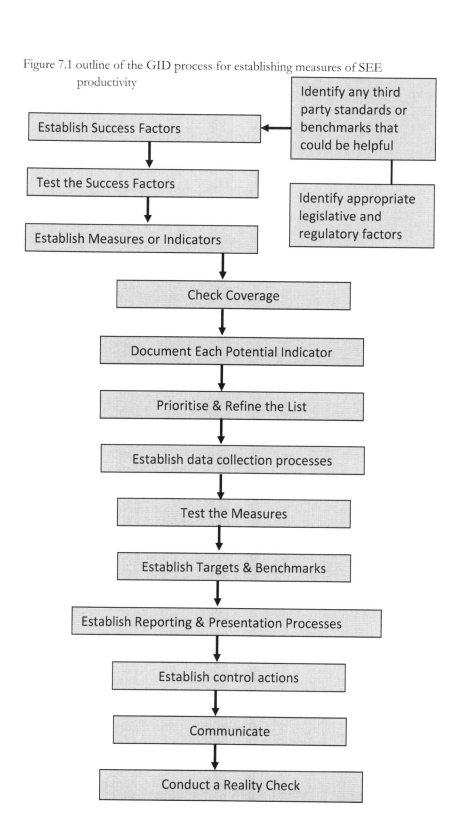

Establish Success Factors

We now know – in concept – what we mean by critical success factors (CSFs) … and we know that for each of them, we need some form of measure or indicator that tells us how well (or badly) we are doing in relation to that factor. Some of these measures and indicators will relate to relatively stable, longer-term factors (key to monitoring performance and maintaining strategic control); others will relate to rapidly-changing, short-term, operational factors (critical to monitoring performance and maintaining operational control). These measures are therefore the key performance indicators (KPIs) and the critical performance indicators (CPIs).

> Critical success factors are the things we have to **do, and do right,** if we are to be successful.
>
> Key and critical performance indicators tell us whether we are getting our critical success factors right.

Collectively the set of measures should tell us how well we are doing against the full set of critical success factors … and, therefore, how likely we are to deliver on our strategy and mission.

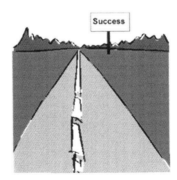

We also know that we have taken a commitment to address all of social, environmental and economic productivity to ensure the longer-term sustainability and well-being of our organisation.

Because firms – and sectors – differ in which factors are important, it is not possible to be prescriptive on what you should measure …. what the success factors are.

All we can say, here, is that you should measure a range of factors that **you** know are important to the future success of your business and that cover all of the SEE productivity factors.

Identify appropriate legislative and regulatory factors and any third party standards or benchmarks that could be helpful

Generally these success factors will be important because you have decided they are … because they determine whether you are meeting the needs and aspirations of your customers (and other stakeholders). Sometimes, however they will be important because someone else says they are – the government, a regulatory agency, a quality agency, a trade association or some other body.

So, it is important that you are aware of any legislation or regulation that you must comply with. (We would hope that as an organisation committed to addressing all of the SEE productivities you are 'ahead of the curve' and meeting levels of performance in excess of those required for mere compliance … but it is, of course, necessary to check. Sector and trade associations are often the best source of advice.)

We have talked previously about the various kinds of standards, best practice guidelines and benchmarks that might offer a useful framework for development. If you decide to adopt one (or more) of these frameworks, there will be obvious implications for the factors you will have to measure.

Figure 7.2 is (hopefully) a helpful checklist to use when trying to identify success factors.

Figure 7.2   Success factors (the things to be measured) can be arrived at:

By considering ...	... and analysing:
1. Social Factors Those factors that impact on the various stakeholder groups, and in particular on employee well-being and performance. 2. Environmental factors Those factors that impact on the external environment, directly or indirectly – energy usage, waste disposed of, carbon footprint, etc. 3. Economic factors Those factors that contribute to the economic and financial well-being of the organisation.	A. Costs All costs – but particularly labour, materials and energy costs. B. Regulatory Issues Here we analyse the major regulatory pressures on the business to find factors that should be added to the 'economic factors' ... recognising that regulatory factors often have short-term and longer-term costs associated with them ... and often have risks that will arise from non-compliance C. Strategic issues Then we look at the mission, and strategic plan to add any issues not uncovered by the first two steps. (This may include additional environmental and social issues) For each of our strategic aims/goals, we should ask: "What area of business or project activity is essential to achieve this goal?" The answers to the question are your candidate CSFs. D. Third party frameworks

Brainstorming is a good means of arriving at a shortlist for further consideration.

Ask the assembled team to spend a few minutes thinking about the issue and writing their individual answers. Then:

- have each person read their own suggestions to the rest of the team
- discuss any differences of opinion
- arrive at a consensus.

The minimum output here is a statement such as:

If we are to achieve long-term success, we have to be particularly good at the following:

1. ....

2. ....

3. ....

... and we would probably be looking to arrive at a list of something like 6 or 7 items covering all three SEE factors.

It is difficult not to include a whole list of factors – especially the 'motherhood and apple pie' factors such as "meeting customer needs" or "recruiting excellent people". Here, the team must go at least one step beyond this level of thinking – to identify those things the organisation needs to do well in order to meet customer needs or recruit good people.

(Sometimes it is difficult for a team to accept that what they are in effect identifying here is not only those things at which the organisation should excel, but also those things where 'average' or 'competent' performance will be OK. If the organisation gets the critical success factors right and does everything else at least competently, success should be assured.)

After working through this process, in addition to 'standard' economic performance factors, a particular organisation might have identified:

- Electricity usage
- Water consumption
- Percentage of suppliers that are ISO 14001 certified
- Number of reportable accidents
- Number of employees participating in community volunteering schemes

.... as factors they regard as important ... because they regard them as important to key stakeholder groups – and especially, directly or indirectly, to customers.

These factors/indicators have to be **really** important. There is little point taking the effort to identify them (and then go on to establish measurement processes) if they are only being used as 'window dressing' ... to pretend to show a commitment to social and environmental issues. They must be seen as being critical to longer-term sustainability and success for the organisation.

When we take these factors forward to create key and critical performance indicators, we will:

- 'touch' all parts of the organisation
- impact on the ability of the senior executive team to plan, to evaluate, to take decisions.

The senior team must be committed to deliver on the project and must show this commitment by the way they talk and act. (i.e. They must 'walk the walk' in addition to 'talking the talk'.)

Test the Success Factors

A management team might establish a project of this kind under a 'banner' such as 'corporate social responsibility'. That's OK – as long as CSR is up-front as a business issue, not sidelined as a "good to do but not critical" initiative.

One way to test this is to go through a process of 'testing' each of the critical success factors for practicality and achievability. We can identify whether CSFs are 'the right ones' by asking:

1. Effectiveness
    - What would happen if we were 'off target' or slightly out of control?
    - How much would that matter?
    - Would it 'reach' the customer?
    - What would the customer think?
    - What might the customer do?"

(and then repeating the analysis by replacing 'customer' with another stakeholder group).

2. Efficiency
    - Can each success factor be incorporated into 'what we do' in a cost-effective manner?

3.   Feasibility

- Are we in control of the drivers that change the success factor? (see below)

Drivers

As potential CSFs are identified, an attempt should be made to understand the drivers (internal and external) that shape and impact upon these CSFs. These are the things that cause the CSF to change. You need to know what it is that moves you in the right direction … and what might occur to throw the proverbial 'spanner in the works'.

The list of CSFs can be categorised … and even, perhaps, grouped or combined, so that we know those that are subject to common drivers. For example, we might have a set of drivers related to Equipment or Skills or ….

This categorisation will depend on the nature of the planning and review process being undertaken: it might be according to the stakeholders group(s) affected; to the processes involved in the measurement or to the specific strategic aims being impacted. By categorising, you might see linkages, overlaps and duplications that allow you to cut the overall number of critical success factors – always a good thing (as long as you maintain comprehensive coverage of all key areas).

Establish measures or indicators for each success factor

The next stage is to list all the things that **could be** counted, measured or assessed and would tell you something about the CSF/driver.

For each of these, give it a 'High', Medium' or 'Low' score dependent on how well it would help you understand good/bad, success/failure, in control/out of control for the CSF … and score it 'High', Medium' or 'Low' in terms of how feasible it would be to count, measure or assess it.

This discussion should lead to a much richer understanding of the issues involved in the measurement process ... and should lead to a shortlist of key performance indicators (KPIs) and critical performance indicators (CPIs) for further, more detailed analysis. (Remember: the difference between a KPI and a CPI is not 'importance' ... but 'criticality' in terms of the frequency of monitoring and the need for fast, responsive action to take control when required.)

The KPIs and CPIs identified or created should be comprehensive – covering all CSFs and/or drivers of those CSFs.

Check coverage of your potential indicators

It is useful to summarise these potential KPIs and CPIs in a chart so that you can see at a glance whether you are covering all of the SEE factors.

So, for the factors we identified above, performance indicators might be:

Indicator	KPI?	CPI?	S	E(nv)	E(con)
Labour hours per tonne	Yes	Yes			X
Energy costs per tonne	Yes	Yes	X	X
Litres of water per tonne	Yes	Yes		X	X
% of suppliers ISO14001 registered	Yes	No		X	
No of reportable accidents	Yes	No	X		
No of employees volunteering	Yes	No	X		

In addition to identifying the factors to be measured, we also have to identify:

- an appropriate measurement frequency
- a data collection process (where data does not currently exist)
- the action(s) to be taken - and the person(s) that should take it - if the measure is off target?

Complete a Performance Indicator Record Sheet for each Indicator

We can use a checklist of things to be considered when creating a performance indicator. Figure 7.2 shows a version filled in for an indicator relating to labour costs.

This shows that the data we use to measure labour cost is collected for other purposes (as part of production control, and to calculate wages). Of course, what this does not show is the nature of the process … and the degree of 'flexibility'/'freedom' we have to make changes.

For example, in relatively high technology processes, the labour costs might be determined by the nature of the process itself (the number of people required to operate machine processes, for example).

(Of course in practice as well as measuring the output and the labour involved, we would almost certainly also be measuring the quality of the Thrimbles produced - to make sure they meet the agreed specification … and perhaps the amount of material used to produce them - so we know how much of our input material we are wasting. This is what we mean by a balanced, set (or family) of measures. For example, if we measure the labour used and find we have used only 14 labour hours per tonne, we might give ourselves a pat on the back. However, if this saving has been at the expense of quality or increased material wastage, we would need to check those measures before we know whether there has been a real, overall improvement.)

Now, let's look at a completed Performance Indicator Specification Sheet relating to energy costs Figure 7-3) .

You will see from this sheet that our measure of energy usage is much less precise; we do not directly measure energy usage on separate production lines or activities, so we have to estimate how much energy is used in any given process. We have chosen to do this on the basis of the proportion of total machine hours that are spent on that particular process. (Without doing some more direct measurement and detective work, it is difficult to know how reliable such an apportionment is, but let us assume that we are fairly confident that this provides data that is useful.)

You will see that we have recognised these limitations and already signalled potential improvements (involving direct metering of energy usage at local levels) … and so the process of specifying such a measure has already made us think about improvements we could make.

You will also notice that we only measure energy usage on a monthly basis, since energy costs do not change very often. (There is no point measuring things frequently if it does not help us control more effectively or improve more readily.)

Performance Indicator Record Sheet: Labour hours per tonne – Thrimble production	
Division/department	D7 Thrimble production
Activity/function being assessed	Manufacture of completed Thrimbles
Title of Indicator	Labour hours per tonne
If it is not clear from the title of the indicator, what actually gets measured/calculated to provide the data for this indicator?	
Person completing this form	Derek Thompson
Date	27th March 2012
Critical success factor(s) which this indicator relates to	Lower selling price
Owner (Person responsible for implementing the indicator)	Lean Manufacturing Black Belt
User (Person responsible for acting on the data)	Thrimble manufacturing team supervisor
What is the source of the data for the indicator?	Production record sheets
Could (should) the data be obtained in any other way?	No – this is a direct computation from two existing measures (labour hours used and tonnes of Thrimbles produced)
How often should the data be collected?	At the end of each shift
Is the reporting process/format clear?	Yes – supervisor prepares a shift summary
Does reporting help the user understand level and trend?	Yes – each summary is added to a cumulative record
Does reporting help the user understand actual versus target performance?	Yes – the summary sheet includes the current target (16 labour hours per tonne)
Are actions prescribed for different levels of the indicator?	Yes – for values within tolerance, below tolerance and above tolerance. (tolerance is target +/- 2)
Is the use of this indicator a cost effective way of maintaining control/progress?	Yes – since the data is recorded for other purposes
Review date	1st Jan 2014

Figure 7-2

Performance Indicator Record Sheet: Energy usage per tonne – Thrimble production	
Division/department	D7 Thrimble production
Activity/function being assessed	Manufacture of completed Thrimbles
Title of Indicator	Energy usage per tonne
If it is not clear from the title of the indicator, what actually gets measured/calculated to provide the data for this indicator?	Energy usage for Thrimble production is calculated by apportioning a share of total energy costs on the basis of the proportion of total machine hours used on Thrimble production
Person completing this form	Derek Thompson
Date	29th March 2012
Critical success factor(s) which this indicator relates to	Lower selling price Carbon Footprint
Owner (Person responsible for implementing the indicator)	Lean Manufacturing Black Belt
User (Person responsible for acting on the data)	Thrimble manufacturing manager
What is the source of the data for the indicator?	Production record sheets Energy invoices
Could (should) the data be obtained in any other way?	Yes – we could measure the energy directly with local energy meters
How often should the data be collected?	At the end of each month
Is the reporting process/format clear?	Yes – Manufacturing manager prepares a monthly summary
Does reporting help the user understand level and trend?	Yes – each summary is added to a cumulative record
Does reporting help the user understand actual versus target performance?	Yes – the summary sheet includes the current target ($4 energy cost per tonne)
Are actions prescribed for different levels of the indicator?	No. The figures form the basis of discussion at the monthly management meeting
Is the use of this indicator a cost effective way of maintaining control/progress?	Unknown, since the costs of direct energy monitoring have not been assessed
Review date	1st Jan 2014

Figure 7-3

Prioritise and refine the list of indicators

We complete a checklist like this for each of our performance indicators ... then, of course, we review them individually – and as a set – against our mission, aims, objectives and critical success factors to ensure we have a balanced, coherent set. We may take out some of the potential measures because the measurement process is too expensive or not feasible technically ... or because another measure gives us enough information about a particular process or activity. For example it may be that one of our proposed CPIs gives us enough advance notice of longer-term performance in a given area, that we can remove one of the proposed KPIs.

We might remove an indicator from the list because we cannot readily identify the control or corrective action that should be taken if the measure is off target. Each of our measures/indicators should be capable of being the cause of fast, responsive action to correct any deviation from plan.

Yet, of course, any such corrective action must not be sub-optimal ... changing the value of one measure positively but having a negative impact on other measures ... unless we are clear that the positive change outweighs any negative change.

The aim of this review is to pare down the list so that we have the minimum number of indicators commensurate with being able to monitor and control all processes and activities that impact on our critical success factors.

Establish data collection processes

For each of our KPIs and CPIs, we must have a data collection process ... so we know what the value of the measure is ... and this data collection process must give us timely data.

Collecting data (rather than relying on feelings and instincts) mean we are working with 'facts' rather than opinions. It is always easier to justify subsequent decision-making when it is based on 'hard' evidence.

Wherever possible, for obvious reasons of convenience and cost, we will use data which is already available – perhaps collected for another purpose. (But remember that you must not distort the measure(s) you intend to use just so you can use already-available data.) Where this is not the case, a specific data collection process must be established and tested.

We have already mentioned that for some indicators, it may not be possible to collect 'hard', quantitative data. For example, measuring customer satisfaction is often done by questionnaires, surveys and focus groups. Though this is 'soft', more qualitative data, we still need to ensure we follow a reliable, structured process to gather the data – a process that can be repeated so that we can subsequently get comparable data,

Where direct data is not available (or the data collection process would be to expensive or too slow), sometimes we can use 'proxy indicators' or measures – so, for example we know the amount of packaging used by simply measuring the packed output levels.

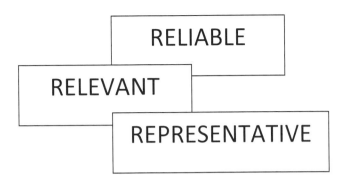

When thinking about data, it is important to remember the "3 R's" that represent the characteristics of 'good' data. Data should be:

- Reliable – it is credible and consistent; the processes by which we manipulate/calculate the data are accurate and consistent over time

- Relevant – it clearly relates to the critical success factor it is designed to help us understand

- Representative – it is typical of the process/function/activity being measured

So, the job of the team is to work through another set of questions.

Where is the data that supports our desired indicator? What is the source of this data we have to collect?

- Does the data already exist? If not, how can it be collected/recorded?
- Who is or should be responsible for collecting the data?
- What is an appropriate measurement frequency? (When do we need to know? How often might it change significantly)

We need to work through these issues and questions until we are confident that we can establish processes that will furnish the data we need to present or build each of our indicators.

Test the Measures

Regardless of how the proposed set of indicators is developed, it should be tested with real data ... first backward (if possible) and then forward.

Backward testing

If the indicators are fairly standard, it might be possible to go back in time and put real historical data into the measures and see if they would have been helpful in offering new insights, missed first time around.

Forward testing

It is also useful to have a 'run-in' period to assess what kind of interpretation problems might crop up. So, the results might be viewed as 'tentative' for the first few cycles and the set of indicators might again be fine-tuned in this period. Assuming our set of KPIs/CPIs makes it through our testing, we should now be relatively confident that we have the basis of a measurement/assessment regime that:

- Ensures we meet all legislative and regulatory requirements
- Covers all of the SEE factors we have identified as important
- Will tell us how well we are doing in making progress towards our strategic goal
- Is practical and feasible

We are half way there!

8   Establishing targets & benchmarks, reporting progress

We are working through the process in Fig 8.1 – and have completed those steps that are greyed out … Fig 8.2 reminds us why we are working through this process of establishing KPIs and CPIs.

There are two main ways you can use KPIs and CPIs to achieve this kind of managerial strength.

Identifying problems and opportunities

The first is to use your KPIs to spot potential problems or opportunities. Remember, your KPIs indicate trends in your business performance. If the trends are moving in the wrong direction, you know you have problems to solve. Similarly, if the trends move consistently in your favour, you may have greater scope for growth than you had previously forecast.

The second is to use your KPIs to set targets throughout your business that will deliver your strategic goals. These may be at the level of divisions or departments, or at process and activity level (and in small organisations may be at the level of the team or individual).

Figure 8.1 outline of the GID process for establishing measures of SEE
productivity

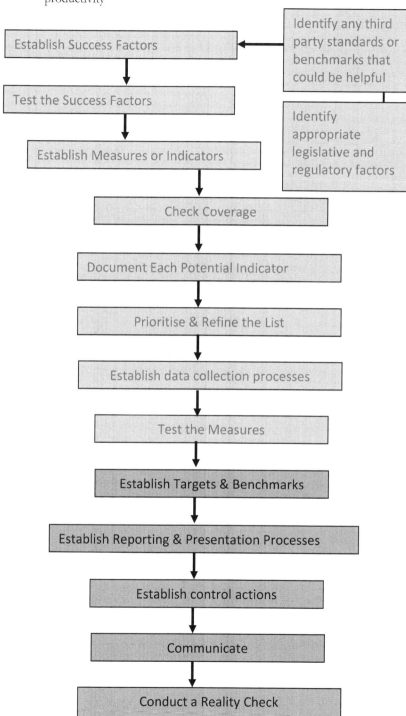

Figure 8-2

Decide whether to opt for internal or external benchmarking

In Chapter 6, we talked about the options of benchmarking between different parts of our own organisation, to identify and the share and spread 'better practice' ... or of benchmarking with other organisations, and hopefully to identify and spread 'best practice'. Making the decision as to whether to adopt internal or external benchmarking has several ramifications – with the main one being the additional work needed to identify potential external benchmark organisations ... and the difficulty of obtaining relevant, reliable data about such organisations.

A summary of the key steps involved in benchmarking is:

1.   Identify what to benchmark and whether to go internal or external

We have identified the indicators and measures we intend to use. Some of these might benefit, in terms of target-setting, by an understanding of 'the art of the possible' and a knowledge of what others are doing. It is unlikely that, even using a relevant benchmarking club, you will be able to find data about all of your potential indicators, so you need to priories those where external knowledge will be most useful .... perhaps where you are less confident that you understand 'success' (see below).

2.   Establish data collection processes

For internal benchmarking, this is the same process for setting the data collection processes for the appropriate indicators.   For external benchmarking, it means you have to identify a source of data – for some indicators, there may be public domain information available; for others it might mean working through a trade association, a friendly, 'sister' company or perhaps a commercial benchmarking club.

3.   Collect data and compare performance

Eventually you will end up with a number of sets of data (minimum of two), but you might have several sets for different companies or different parts of your own organisation. Comparing this data enables you to identify performance gaps – where external organisations are better than you are ... or where some parts of your organisation outperform others.

4.   Set targets

These performance gaps allow you to set meaningful and credible targets – not necessarily making up all of the gap in one step, but perhaps by establishing 'milestones' – intermediate targets that move you (or move the underperforming parts of your organisation) towards the 'better' or 'best' practice.

Defining success (and failure) or compliance

For key performance indicators you should establish a target or benchmark which represents where you want to be – 'success'. If the timescale to get to 'best in class' or some other benchmark is long, you might set an intermediate target for the next measurement period.

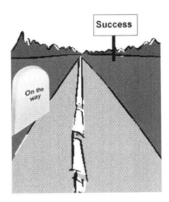

For each of your critical performance indicators, you should establish a target or benchmark that represents 'compliance' – processes are on track and no corrective action is required.

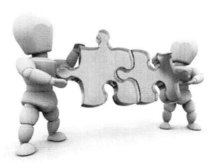

For both KPIs and CPIs, you might also establish a 'lower limit' that represents 'failure' – something that not only means that performance is unacceptable but signals that critical decisions/actions might have to follow.

You will almost certainly set targets based on a combination of past performance and expectations/aspirations arising from the strategy/planning process ... and, of course, you might be assisted through the use of benchmarking data. Even if you have not adopted a formal, benchmarking process you should have an understanding of market and competitor positions ... and you therefore can undertake 'informal benchmarking'.

This is particularly important for your social and environmental indicators, where you might have little past experience of measurement and target setting. You might have to work with organisations that do have some knowledge and/or experience – government and non-governmental support agencies ... or external consultants.

The aim should be to set targets or establish benchmarks which are challenging but realistic. You might, for some of your success factors, aspire to a 'perfection target' (100% customer satisfaction, zero defects, 100% recycling of packaging, etc) but such aspirations might not be practical in the short-term. (You therefore might have such targets as longer-term aims but you should then have realistic, time-bound milestone targets on the way to such perfection.)

All targets should be:

• clear;
• quantified; and
• time-bound.

i.e. you should know what you aim to do and by when.

So … the target:

To ship at least 90% of orders within 3 days of receiving the order

.. is a valid aim … but not a valid target, since from reading this target we do not know whether the organisation intends to achieve this level of performance in the next week, the next 3 months or the next 3 years.

Conflicting Targets

Because you have got a 'balanced' set of success factors (covering social, environmental and economic factors), some of your targets might be in conflict.

A programme of activity to reach one goal might impact negatively on the achievement of another. For example, by aiming for a challenging environmental target, you might incur higher costs … which might impact negatively on a financial target.

This is why you have a 'system' of interlinked success factors and associated performance indicators … and why the senior team must be committed to all of the targets. (Otherwise it soon becomes apparent which of the targets has 'real' commitment … and therefore becomes the focus of real attention.)

Establish effective forms of reporting and presentation

We must establish reporting mechanisms for each indicator … and for the set of indicators, making sure that those who need to use the data get that data when, where and how they need it.

Since the purpose of measurement is to help make improvement happen, the frequency of reporting depends on how often it is appropriate to intervene in the process under review.

On a factory floor, measures might be taken every minute because the particular machine might be capable of near instantaneous adjustment. The individual members of a family of measures - at factory floor level - might be summarised and reviewed on a daily basis and the balanced family might be reviewed weekly.

At departmental or divisional levels, individual measures might be made and reviewed weekly, and the balanced family reviewed every two weeks or monthly.

At senior, organisational levels, some individual measures would probably be taken no more than monthly with the aggregated set of measures reviewed less frequently - perhaps quarterly at board meetings. In exceptional cases, for specific projects, measurement might be more frequent - say, weekly - but generally major corporate programmes cannot afford that many checkpoints.

However, when we are talking about 'critical' performance indicators. It is likely that many of these will be reported frequently ... to maintain the 'feel' for performance that senior managers need.

We are looking at the kind of indicators that the CEO will want to know about regularly ... so weekly reporting of CPIs is probably the minimal position ... but many of the CPIs will be reported more often. A good starting point is to consider four main frequencies – real time (or near real time), daily, weekly and monthly and to determine which should apply for any specific measure according to the likely change in the value over those reporting frequency periods, and the likelihood of control action being necessary in that period.

Level and Trend

The data collected and its frequency of presentation should be enough for managers to be able to establish both level (what is the current value of the particular indicator) and trend (is it moving up or down … signifying better or worse performance … and is this movement consistent). It is no use looking at an 'improvement' in the indicator and thinking "We are doing well" if the longer-term trend is downward.

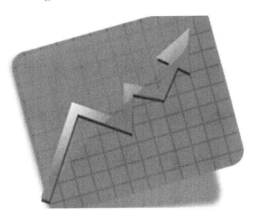

If the trend is downward, then we know we have problems to solve. Conversely, if the trend is upwards it doesn't just mean that all is well … it also means that we might have greater scope for growth than we had previously forecast.

Dashboards

Performance dashboards/executive dashboards have become popular over recent years. They present performance data in easily accessible/readable formats … perhaps as traffic light indicators (where 'problem' indicators – those whose value is below or above a 'trigger limit' - are shown in red) or as dials, bar graphs, etc.

The (very sensible) aim is to show a lot of information simply and to allow managers to concentrate on 'management by exception'.

However there are advantages and disadvantages to such forms of reporting. The advantages are clear but such highly aggregated displays can:

• over-simplify … and lead to less discriminating judgement from those reading the data;
• fail to show trends … and many performance indicators only deliver their true value when they are charted and presented as a time-series.

The main issue is to make sure that the data are presented clearly, making good use of charts, diagrams and other visual forms of presentation. Focus on:

• The reader
• The information the reader needs
• The action that the reader needs to take based on the information

This is more important for critical performance indicators than for key performance indicators since for CPIs, the information has to be assimilated and action taken more quickly.

At the shop-floor, real-time level, the 'presentation' of a CPI may be in the form of a machine alarm going off. For a KPI at the strategic level, the presentation may be in the form of a monthly graph of performance data.

Establish Control Actions

We report so that people can take action. So we have to decide on what kind of action should be taken (and by whom) if any of our indicators show we are off target?

In effect, our targets (or perhaps intermediate points on the way to our targets) become trigger points and we identify the actions to be taken when those trigger points are reached.

This is far more important for our critical performance indicators where need to take action swiftly before the poor performance results in loss or damage. Each of our CPIs should be capable of being the cause of fast, responsive action to correct any deviation from plan. Yet, of course, any such corrective action must not be sub-optimal ... changing the value of one measure positively but having a negative impact on other measures ... unless we are clear that the positive change outweighs any negative change.

Our KPIs, too, should result in corrective action – but here, because of the timespan of reporting and action, there may be time for consideration, reflection and discussion before such corrective action is determined. For the CPIs the corrective action should be pre-programmed.

If this alarm goes off, do this.

If the quality level drops below X%, do this.

In each case it must be clear as to:

- What the level of the indicator is that triggers the action
- What the action is
- Who takes it
- When they take it

For example, the action might be taken immediately or at the end of the current batch, the current job, the current shift or ...

The 'lower' the level at which such action takes place, the better … as it normally has a faster effect. These 'actions' (or perhaps more properly 'reactions') must be determined in partnership with those who will take such actions and must be done in concert with designing the presentation method for the data.

Communicate

Once we are confident that we have an effective set of performance indicators that will help us control the factors we have identified as critical to our success, and we have determined the actions to be taken when the data indicates some form of 'error' condition, we should communicate this information throughout the organisation.

Not everyone needs to know about or understand all of the factors but everyone who has some potential impact or influence on any one of the indicators does need to know:

(a)   what the measure/indicator is
(b)   why it is important
(c)   who is measuring it and how often
(d)   who receives the information
(e)   who takes action based on the indicator

and, most importantly …

(f)   what their particular role is in relation to this indicator.

In all sorts of processes, and in all sorts of books, the importance of communication is stressed. Yet, in those same books it is often held up to be a 'problem', something that does not happen as it should.

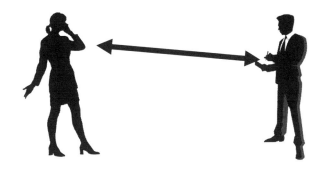

Effective communication depends most strongly on a will to communicate but it also requires the person 'broadcasting' to:

• Understand the 'audience' and tailor the form and language of the communication to the audience
• To get feedback from the audience that enables a judgement to be made as to whether the communication has been effective ...

... and it requires all of those involved in the measurement and management process to continually reinforce the importance of the indicators in what they do!

Conduct a Reality Check

When we think we have our measurement, reporting, communication and action processes in place, we should stop for a moment and make sure we have got the basics right. We should then check that for each of our indicators:

Everyone knows it matters

Everyone knows who is responsible

Everyone knows what is 'good' and what is 'bad'

Measuring and reporting it should allow timely correction/improvement intervention

Measuring and reporting it should change behaviour/outcomes

This is the last check before we go 'live' – so we must be sure that the set of indicators we have selected (and tested) is going to do the job we want done.

So there is a list of final questions to ask.

1. Are we leaving out something significant?

If the measures have been designed to fit with the strategic plan (and they should have been), this is almost a test of the plan itself. Sometimes local managers introduce measures relating to a pet project or to issues which may not be 'strategic'. For example, a manager may be concerned about absenteeism in his/her own department ... and will therefore introduce a measure relating to absenteeism into the family of measures at his/her level. This is not a problem ... indeed it may be quite sensible ... unless introducing this measure 'forces out' a measure that does relate to a more strategic issue.

Concepts that are contained in the strategic plan but which are difficult to measure may also be omitted. An advertising agency may measure billings, renewals and market share quite easily. However its plan may suggest they want to improve creativity. How do they measure it? If its in the plan, it should be measured .... even if this means using surrogate data - such as awards received - or external survey data.

2. Are the measures inconsistent with individual motivations?

So, we agree on what we want!

Since you do, indeed, get what you measure, it is important to co-ordinate group and individual measures. Periodic, individual appraisals are rarely well-handled by organisations; they often reflect antiquated, formal specifications and processes that do not reflect current practices or concerns. If machine operators are now involved in a world of computer-based diagnostics and control, their evaluation should not - as it often is - be based on length of service, absenteeism and their knowledge of hand tools.

No matter how dominant the team ethic has become, it is still the individual who shows up for work and contributes new ideas. We need to ensure that performance measures reflect the interests and concerns of the individuals -as well as the groups - involved.

We now have a 'system' that ensures that we know how we are doing, and a process that ensures we take action when that system tells us things are not on plan.

3. Are the proper authority, tools and training available to ensure accurate measurement?

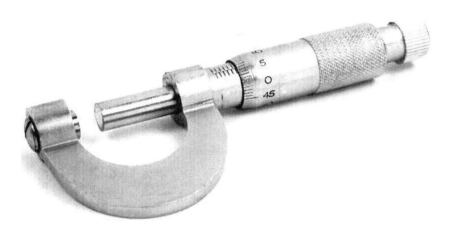

The elements of the family of measures at any level must be reasonably controllable by the people operating at that level. However, if the basic concept of a product or service is faulty, no amount of teamwork or individual effectiveness will save the day. When you measure a poorly designed process, you are sure to obtain poor results.

For an example, most of us get really annoyed when telemarketers call us when we are having dinner. The chances of making a sale at that time are almost zero. The marketers assigned to the dinnertime slot should call another time zone or simple rebel ... the basic service design does not allow them to be successful.

In one factory, operators were each running several machines side by side. Measurement revealed slow processing and flawed products. It turned out that after the machines had been running a while, small leaks had developed and dripped onto the floor. Operators simple walked around these small puddles, barely noticing them until an operator from another part of the plant pointed them out. Drip pans were provided and the processing speeded up. Subsequently all of the operators were trained in Total Productive Maintenance and the machines were taken apart and re-sealed. This eliminated a number of minor problems that had collectively been robbing the line of both quality and speed. (This is a good example of a performance indicator NOT being used as the basis of performance improvement – it was only the intervention of the interested operator that caused the improvement to happen. Something, therefore, was wrong with the overall 'system' of measurement – most likely that those involved were not convinced of the real importance of the measurements being taken.)

4.   **Can the measures be updated as necessary?**

A set of indicators should be reviewed regularly (probably each year unless something happens which forces an earlier review) to ensure that it still fits the current strategic interests of the organisation.

A well-designed set of indicators strikes a balance among several measures whilst maintaining a creative tension among them because of choices or tradeoffs forced between different elements - quality and cost, timeliness and documentation, etc. Over time this tension can be dissipated because the organisation has learnt to live with a particular set of measures and knows which to ignore (because the real priority is ...). In this case, the family of measures should be reviewed and probably adjusted.

5. Are the rewards consistent with group rewards and recognition?

Incentive schemes measuring only labour productivity survive in many industries ... even where labour cost is a small part of overall cost. There are also group recognition systems that identify 'team of the month' but are based on some trivial internal team process rather than on team outcomes reflected in the set of performance indicators.

If the set of indicators does not seem helpful to a team, they often invent their own ... and embark on what they feel are helpful activities such as speeding up the line or improving quality ... but they might address the problem sub-optimally - speeding up the line to the detriment of quality, for example.

Though we want 'empowered' employees, we want that empowerment working in the right directions - as dictated by the 'official' family of measures. People therefore need to understand - and see the sense in - the official measures.

When, as here, a group or family of measures is involved, reward and recognition should come not from achieving success against one measure ... but, wherever possible, against a number of measures in the family. It is the job of the senior team to resolve potential conflicts between individual measures such that overall performance, measured against the 'basket of measures', represents an upward trend.

6.   Do the measures foster good customer and supplier relations?

Does the family of measures make sense to internal and external customers and to the suppliers of the group in question? (In an ideal world, customers and suppliers would have been involved in designing appropriate measures.)

Well-meaning individuals who assume they know what customers and suppliers want can be dangerous. For example, a manager who learns that some customers are annoyed with late deliveries might work very hard to get all orders delivered as soon as possible. However, for some (many?) customers, an early delivery might be as inconvenient as a late one; there may be a particular 'window of delivery' to hit.

The only way to understand customer and supplier needs and concerns is to talk to them - and to talk often.

If you can satisfy yourself that you can answer all these questions appropriately, you seem to have a sound set of KPIs and CPIs ready to go.

9 Where do we go from here?

This is a good time to be writing this book. The recent economic crisis is leading many to question 'the way things are done' ... to question whether 20th century forms of business are suitable for the 21st century.

Nordhaus and Tobin, of Yale university, wrote as long ago as 1972 that:

"GDP is not a measure of welfare. The GDP is simply a gross tally of everything produced in the US- products and services, good things and bad." (Nordhaus and Tobin, 1972).Since then it seems to have got a lot clearer to many that GDP measures economic activity but is not necessarily an effective measure of the value provided to society by that economic activity ... and it has certainly become clearer since 1972 that GDP does indeed, as Nordhaus and Tobin said back then, include 'bad' things (like pollution and environmental damage) and often leads to other 'bad' things (like increasing wealth differentials and increased social damage).

We have seen a number of brave experiments at creating alternative forms of business; and we have seen mainstream business begin to explore and experiment with issues outside of financial success.

Perhaps this questioning of current practice together with the range of experiments we have seen are creating the 'perfect storm' for a real step change in how mainstream business considers and addresses what it does on a more holistic basis – and starts to build in primary consideration of social and environmental issues as part of business decision-making.

Perhaps we can get away from short-term economic focus by organisations (all that matters is our next quarterly set of figures) and governments (all that matters is the next election) and create policy and practice that aims at longer-term.

References

Nordhaus, W and Tobin, J. 1972
"Is growth obsolete?"
in Economic Growth, National Bureau of Economic Research Series No.
96E. New York: Columbia University Press.

INDEX

social productivity, iii, v, viii, 8, 15, 21, 22, 23, 24, 25, 30, 41, 42, 43, 44, 45, 66, 69, 83, 84, 85, 86, 88, 95

sustainability, iii, v, 13, 14, 15, 29, 32, 37, 66, 68, 81, 83, 87, 88, 93, 112, 115

triple bottom line, 10

World Confederation of Productivity Science, i, 11, 17, 68, 153

ABOUT THE AUTHORS

The authors of Measuring & Improving Social, Environmental and Economic Productivity: Getting It Done are Mike Dillon & John Heap

Professor Mike Dillon is Technical Director of the Institute of Productivity and is a world-renowned expert on manufacturing strategy and on the seafood sector. Mike has worked with United Nations agencies for over 20 years – either writing best practice guides or designing and leading projects in developing countries. Recently Mike has been involved in a number of major international projects, working with the United Nations Industrial Development Organisation.

Mike is Vice-President of the World Network of Productivity Organizations; a Fellow of the World Academy of Productivity Science; Senior Research Fellow at Grimsby Institute in the UK; and Secretary of IAFI, the association of seafood professionals.

Mike has been invited onto the board of a leading green technology firm – Clean Green Pallet Company – and will act as their corporate social responsibility director.

Contact Mike at mike@instituteofproductivity.com

John Heap is Managing Director of the Institute of Productivity; President of the World Confederation of Productivity Science; President of the European Association of National Productivity Centres; visiting professor at Srinivas Institute of Management Studies in Mangalore, India; co-editor of the International Journal of Productivity & Performance Management; a Member of Council of the Institute of Management Services; a Member of the

Advisory Board of the Institute for Consultancy and Productivity Research (India); and a director of Juice e-Learning.

John has been involved in a number of recent international projects working with the United Nations Industrial Development Organisation.

John, like Mike, is the author of a number of books and journal articles and a regular keynote presenter at international conferences.

Contact John at john@instituteofproductivity.com

World Confederation of
Productivity Science

European Association of National
Productivity Centres

15616550R00096

Made in the USA
San Bernardino, CA
01 October 2014